ABOUT THE AUTHOR

Rona Cran is a London-based writer and scholar. They teach North American poetry at the University of Birmingham, and are the founding co-director of the Network for New York School Studies, which advocates for, supports, and emphasizes the value of community-based public poetry initiatives. Their first book, *Collage in Twentieth-Century Art, Literature, and Culture: Joseph Cornell, William Burroughs, Frank O'Hara, and Bob Dylan*, was published in 2014.

'The scaffolding of Cran's memory, in sensory, quotidian, vivid detail. A family album, a romp of associative time. Moments of quixotic motion in a litany of heartbeats. Joe Brainard's classic form is a lifeline here for the care and power of grief.'
- **Anne Waldman**

'Never has Joe Brainard's pioneering format been put to more haunting, heart-breaking use than in *I Remember Kim*. This kaleidoscopic elegy movingly explores the complex, double-edged compensations of memory, oscillating between vibrant vignettes of sisterly love and bleak, serial snapshots of the onslaught of grief. A tour de force.' - **Mark Ford**

'Rona Cran's *I Remember Kim* lovingly honors the form of Joe Brainard's legendary book-length list poem by fusing it with her vivid remembrances of her younger sister Kim, whom she lost to diabetes at the tragic young age of thirty-two in the middle of our global pandemic. Deliberate in its achronology, Cran's seven hundred thirty strophes nevertheless seek to embody the "nearly thirty three years….that Kim was in {her} life", a bond forged by an unforgettable third and fourth culture childhood, then bolstered in adulthood by a mutual restlessness and love of continuous travel, especially to Lake Bogoria, Coiba, and Town Beach at Sunset; of Dolly Parton lyrics and the poems of Danez Smith; of the philosophy of Doris Lessing, and stories by Chimamanda Adichie and David Sedaris; of hair mascara, and cats named Uncle Maj and Chui. "The joy/is not/the same/without/the/pain", fellow Briton Damon Gough sang once in a popular British romantic comedy directed by an American. So, too, does Cran sweetly remind this reader that beside such devastating loss walk responses like wonder and pride—over her sister's unconditional loyalty to family, her compassion for humanity, and her steadfast light. Unguarded in its mess and message, I Remember Kim proves a heartfelt and engaging memoir buoyed by Cran's resolve "not to master" but "navigate {through} grief", and with a brio equal to the work of her idols Joe Brainard, Georges Perec, and David Wojnarowicz.'
- **Paolo Javier**

I Remember Kim
a memoir of grief
(after Joe Brainard)

Rona Cran

PUBLISHED BY VERVE POETRY PRESS
https://vervepoetrypress.com
mail@vervepoetrypress.com

All rights reserved
© 2023 Rona Cran

The right of Rona Cran to be identified as author of this work has been asserted in accordance with section 77 of the Copyright, Designs and Patents Act 1988.

No part of this work may be reproduced, stored or transmitted in any form or by any means, graphic, electronic, recorded or mechanical, without the prior written permission of the publisher.

FIRST PUBLISHED SEPTEMBER 2023

Printed and bound in the UK
by ImprintDigital, Exeter

ISBN: 978-1-913917-38-8

Cover: Kim with manta, Socorro, 2018. Photograph © Xaime Beiro

*For Kim
and
for Freya*

PREFACE

'You cannot sit motionless in the heart of these perils, because the boat is rocking like a cradle, and you are pitched one way and the other, without the slightest warning'
- Herman Melville

On October 18th, 2021, my little sister Kim died suddenly, at night, from complications relating to Type 1 diabetes, complications which I still don't quite understand. She was 32. She was found lying on the floor by her bed, by her boss, who went to investigate when she didn't show up for work. That morning, her boss had already encountered death – a turtle, lying in shallow surf. Kim was blonde, slender, her ears full of piercings. No tattoos, just a scar on her right shin that she told people was the result of a snakebite. Her eyes were blue. Her middle name was Ross – our dad's middle name – and was given to her because she was the youngest of three daughters and no boychild ever materialised. She had a few freckles, and she tanned more easily than either me or our sister Sophie. She lived in Santa Catalina, in Panama. She loved cats and whale sharks. She was a scuba diving instructor. Although we had not seen each other for six months, we were in almost daily contact.

This small book is an attempt to give shape to my grief. I borrow its form from Joe Brainard, an artist and poet who in the early 1970s published *I Remember*, a powerful book-length prose poem consisting of around fifteen hundred 'recollections'. There have been other *I Remembers*, including Georges Perec's, Margo Glantz's, Lee Ann Brown's, and Denis Hirson's. This is mine.

At heart, *I Remember Kim* is what its title suggests – a memoir about my sister. It's a collage of memories covering the thirty-two, nearly thirty-three, years that she was in my life, from the day that she was born to the night she died. Inevitably, then, it's also about others – our parents, our sister Sophie, our friends, her friends, my friends, her colleagues, my colleagues, my partner, my cats, her cats, my students, the people I encountered in the wake of her death. We were born and grew up in Kenya; we went to secondary school and university in England; she travelled the world and ultimately settled in Panama, more or less, where she died; I settled in London, where she also lived for a time. So it's about these places too, and about how we navigated our close friendship and sisterhood and shared aunty-hood from afar, and in the usual ways (long-anticipated visits and hilarious drunken catch-ups, endless phone calls, photographs, and the sharing of baby animal memes and one-star film reviews).

I Remember Kim is also, to borrow David Wojnarowicz's subtitle from *Close to the Knives* (1991), a memoir of disintegration, the dissolution I felt in the days, weeks, and months after her death embodied or enacted in its relentless and fragmentary form, and in the fact that it does not know if it is a poem or a memoir or a letter or something else. As much as it is a coming-together of memories, so it is also a falling-apart – it is about the failure of memory, of memories, of memoir. It is about how to remember when all you want to do is forget. It is about what happens when your entire past, present, and future are reconfigured in an instant – in a phone call neither caller nor recipient will ever be able to forget. 'Memory', as Marita Sturken writes, 'establishes life's continuity; it gives meaning to the present, as each moment is constituted by the past'. Kim's death altered all my memories: a constant in my life, I now feel her absence even in recollecting moments or events in which she was not present. As Brad Gooch writes, 'I'm not nostalgic, just shocked'. She is an ever-present absence; an ever-absent presence. To remember, in this way, is to be haunted. And more, my memories of her feel inexhaustible – they can never be used up – and yet for all that I remember they are not and never can be up to the task of conveying who she was and how I felt about her, and how I feel about her now, in my role as one of two 'surviving' sisters, 'surviving' daughters. What have I forgotten? In what ways has my memory failed? To slightly reformulate *Star Trek* via Emily St. John Mandel, *I Remember Kim* is about learning, in painfully multifaceted ways, the insufficiency of survival. And in writing about my sister in this way, I offer a treatise, of sorts, on a particular kind of grief that has felt obscured or neglected or unspoken or insufficiently acknowledged: each grief is its own landscape, fundamentally un-chartable, but there are very few memoirs by bereaved siblings.

In order to live, then, I wrote this short book, this long poem, this memoir, this poetic letter to my sister. Writing it was a physical process, a bodily as much as an emotional exercise. I wrote it piecemeal, by hand, in a notebook given to me by a friend, over many months, on many train journeys, sticking more or less to Joe Brainard's method in order to overcome my inability to concentrate for long periods of time and my sense of having lost control ('No one / to witness / and adjust, no one to drive the car', as William Carlos Williams wrote), as well as what often felt like the catastrophic failure of language in the context of my grief. Brainard's poetic formula enacts the possibility of fantastical temporal and affective slippage – released from the bonds of chronology and narrative and place, I felt as if I could move mercurially and without rationale through time and through emotion, from the banal to the paradigm-shifting, the personal to the cultural, recollecting the past with a clarity and specificity that astonished me, whilst also enacting the creation of new memories, fabricated out of the immediate, agonising present, in order to navigate, rather than master, my grief.

***

I Remember Kim

I remember when you were born. You are my first memory. I was four. While there has been, and will be, life for me after you, there was none at all before. Driving to the War Memorial Hospital in Nakuru, to meet you, I remember Cheryl turning to the four of us (we were crammed in the back seat of her station wagon) and saying: 'Thank God it's a girl – we wouldn't want any boys around here!' And there never were. You were the fifth member of our gang. You are. When Bella arrived, she made six. You made us Cran girls a three.

Three sisters. Three – the magic number. Three witches. The power of three. A triangle: the strongest shape. Three sisters: 'the tenderest, toughest place on earth'. I remember mum saying that our threeness made us a little team, a gang, identifying as adjacent to, sometimes in opposition to, her and dad. Before you came, though I don't remember it, it was one parent per child, interchangeably. After, it was us and them, or us or them, or us versus them. We three against the world.

I remember 'When shall we three meet again?'

I remember 'Who is the third who always walks beside you?'

I remember that one of the first things I thought, or felt, when Sophie told me you had been found 'without a heartbeat' or 'without a pulse' (I don't remember which, I do remember which), was that I don't know how to *be*, not in a three.

I remember, after she told me, feeling as if I'd gone deaf, partially. As if my head were under water. This continued for several hours, perhaps even into the next day (I don't remember), and intermittently ever since – a low, intense, internal throb as if my heart were beating inside my own head.

I remember that I had a headache for a month, no let-up.

I remember: everything has changed.

I remember: it should have been me.

I remember that I didn't sleep that night. Not for a moment. That I read Doris Lessing's *The Golden Notebook*. That I found some headphones and listened to the Big Read recording of *Moby Dick*, which seemed appropriate. One of the chapters was about catching and killing a whale; the next about two men urging the sharks eating the body of the whale to be quieter and somehow more godly as they ate.

I remember that I spent that night trying to relive our lives together, right from that first memory, in order, onwards.

I remember partially succeeding, whilst also recognizing that memory just doesn't work like that.

Things that I remembered that night included:

- schooldays: me sneaking into mum's flat at lunchtime to eat sugar (brown, thickly granulated) and finding, when you and I met guiltily by the sugar caddy one afternoon, that you did the exact same thing;

- you riding Cloud, me riding Boy, hacking through the fields that surrounded the school;

- you falling over a horse jump, aged five, and breaking your arm, and me refusing to believe you;

- Dolla and I teaching you to walk ('come to me, Bimble');

- you being diagnosed with Type I diabetes, aged eleven, and mum telling me about it over the phone, from 4000 miles away. I remember how it (I was told) explained how skinny you'd gotten, and how thirsty you always were; how it was treatable (nobody told me you could die from it); how much I cried in my room at the top of School House, and how kind my roommate and house mistress both were.

- you and me walking down Brick Lane one evening, one of us clutching a bottle of red, and being mistaken for twins.

I remember that the last thing I ever cooked for you – apart from the slice of toast I made for you on the morning you left – was chilli. Vegetarian – split red lentils and chipotle chilli flakes; with rice and Oatly crème fraiche. That we drank red wine with it, even though you had to be up early to catch your flight. That we pulled our slightly rickety Ercol dining table into the middle of the room and covered it with the red, green, and yellow cloth that Martin and I had bought in Sodwana Bay. I can't remember if we lit candles – probably. I remember that we made Meera Sodha's chia seed brownies for dessert, and that we reminisced (competitively) about how amazing *your* brownies were.

I remember that on the day after you died – a Tuesday – I made the same meal. Only no wine, this time, and no brownies. One year later, on the day that is now 'your anniversary', I made it again.

I remember that now you have a deathday, as well as a birthday.

I remember that Dolla called me as I cooked. I remember that she said, in a small voice and through tears: 'we've lost one of our gang'.

I remember that I could still eat then.

I remember making green tea, after Sophie called, and sitting on the sofa to drink it (Martin and me) in the 'disgathering light' (O'Hara).

I remember, a workaholic like you, thinking I'd be fine to go to work.

I remember thinking: 'I need to do this on my own'. And: 'I need to be by myself'. And: 'I need to *be* myself'.

I remember that we walked, Martin and I. The afternoon was misty and damp. The clocks had yet to change. We went out through the back gate, past Bina's flat, where she was cleaning something in the kitchen. For the first time in my life, I didn't want to talk to her. I didn't know how. We crossed the roads you need to cross to reach the Greenway. We didn't say very much.

I remember wanting to jump on the next plane to Panama.

I remember the agony of thinking of you being alone, lying on a slab somewhere.

I remember how much I wanted to hold you.

I remember you saying you wanted to be buried at sea ('like Bin Laden' – you said that, and I said it again when we scattered your ashes many months later, and no one laughed but me). I remember that Sophie expressed surprise that you and I had talked about our deaths.

I remember that you and me and Martin had often talked about what we'd like to happen to our bodies after death: for Martin it was the fiery helter-skelter, me riding on his back into the flames, or being left in a thicket in Mile End Cemetery. For me, the Parsi Towers of Silence, or a version of this, something involving tall trees, fresh air, and carrion birds.

I remember that I never took you to Mile End Cemetery – that you will never see the flowers there, or hear the birds, or, in the snow, help find a lost dog called Ruby.

I remember 'lost at sea'.

I remember walking, with Martin, by the water, around and beneath the Olympic Stadium. My head was full of poetry.

I remember: 'is the / earth as full as life was full, of them?' (O'Hara)

I remember:
> *the only thing to do is simply continue*
> *is that simple*
> *yes, it is simple because it is the only thing to do*
> *can you do it*
> *yes, you can because it is the only thing to do* (O'Hara).

I remember:
> *The stars are not wanted now; put out every one,*
> *Pack up the moon and dismantle the sun,*
> *Pour away the ocean and sweep up the wood;*
> *For nothing now can ever come to any good* (Auden).

I remember 'No one / to witness / and adjust, no one to drive the car' (Williams).

I remember: 'Get thee to a nunnery' (Shakespeare).

I remember wondering about – and looking into – the possibility of repatriating your body.

I remember thinking how much you'd hate being brought back to England – to the dark and the rain of October – even though (especially because?) you were dead.

I remember wondering what you looked like, dead. And what they would do to you if you had to be repatriated.

I remember wondering about – and looking into – the possibility of burial at sea.

I remember the failure of language: how the past tense, and

words like 'cremation', 'body', and 'death certificate' remain profoundly unsayable.

I remember the success of language too: how messages prefaced with 'there are no words' inevitably gave way to moving, wise, and capacious tributes to you.

I remember 'trying to understand how a person vanishes' (Notley).

I remember how beautiful the skies were in the days after you died; how the autumn was coming on, and how I'd always liked talking to you about it, about the beauty we found in this drab, often grey, place.

I remember telling you about starling murmurations, and how you and mum went and saw one happening, one January during the pandemic, in the Somerset dusk.

I remember recommending books to you – mostly poor recommendations, as far as recommendations go, of books you either didn't get or didn't like, books you would 'accidentally' abandon in airports around the world.

I remember us recommending films and TV shows to each other, with more success: often horrors, or psychological thrillers, often in Spanish. These included:
- *The Devil's Backbone*
- *Los Ojos de Julia*
- *Pan's Labyrinth*
- *La Casa de Papel*
- *REC.*

I remember that we were going to make our own horror movie, the product of years of in-jokes, encounters with creepy people, and strange nocturnal experiences. After a man approached us on the steps leading back up to the house we used to stay in at the coast, at Vipingo, holding out a giant fish and explaining in a hoarse voice: 'it is called the grouper', we even had the title. It was going to be called *The Grouper*. I remember that we'll never get to make it.

I remember watching a horror movie – *The Night House* – a few weeks after you died, and thinking that I heard your voice in the flat. Quite loud, quite normal-sounding, and definitely you. I don't remember what you said – nothing of significance.

I remember 'I was afraid to put out my hand, for fear it would touch nothing, or to speak, for fear no one would answer' (Marilynne Robinson).

I remember that almost all the books I read in the weeks and months after you died were horrors, or near-horrors. I think you would have enjoyed all of them (I'm probably wrong). These included:
- *A Head Full of Ghosts* by Paul Tremblay
- *The Last House on Needless Street* by Catriona Ward
- *The Whistling* by Rebecca Netley
- *The Only Good Indians* by Stephen Graham Jones
- *Reprieve* by James Han Mattson
- *Leave the World Behind* by Rumaan Alam
- *Our Wives Under the Sea* by Julia Armfield
- *Things We Lost in the Fire* by Mariana Enriquez
- *Paradise* by Toni Morrison
- *Where I End* by Sophie White.

I remember saying goodbye to you – April 11th, 2021, a Sunday. I remember waving at the darkened windows of your Uber as you were driven away to Heathrow in the early spring morning.

I remember you and me, on the phone, in the pandemic: 'Open the pubs! Open the pubs!'

I remember that no one can make me laugh like you can (could). Apart from Martin. The two of you *together*... oh boy.

I remember Christmas together (you, me, Martin): drinking wine from the carafe you bought us, and hacking up the dining table with a kitchen knife that was never the same again (neither was the table). I wish we still had the table.

I remember that you supplied us with two exceptional carafes.

I remember your Christmas with the Colombians.

I remember all the bars where you worked, some of which no longer exist: Albert&Pearl, Ladybird, Barrios North and South, the St. Martin's Lane Hotel, the sleazy banker bar in the city where punters would buy whole bottles of champagne that they wouldn't drink, somewhere French in Soho, ninetyeight bar on Curtain Road. I map the bar crawl in my mind for when we are stronger.

I remember cocktails: old fashioneds (muddled for the appropriate time or not at all), negronis (the bartenders' cocktail), Thames Waters (bespoke, made by you for us), espresso Martinis.

I remember coke, and Halloween costumes (hated), and the time you got one of your rings bent out of shape and stuck on your finger so tightly your finger turned purple (now I wear that ring on a silver chain).

I remember playing squash. I remember always planning to play tennis.

I remember our plans to go baseball-batting, axe-throwing, furniture-smashing.

I remember the idea of 'the rage room'.

I remember piercings. I remember Eclipse, in Camden – the basement studio with the cheap, deep, leather couches that were impossible to get up out of; the glass cabinets full of punk metal jewellery; the beautiful French owner with the huge breasts, full-body tattoos, and cute little daughter; her apprentice, who became the piercing sorcerer, and came to know us well. I remember how your blood sugar would always plummet after a piercing. Sitting on the deep, cheap, leather sofas, your hands shaking, drinking pink Lucozade. How we had to pay cash. How you never admitted you were diabetic when you filled out the waiver form. How cartilage piercings crunch, but don't really hurt. How mine always took way longer to heal than yours. How I was always playing catch-up to you, in terms of numbers of piercings ('always room for more', you would say). How we always went for lunch or cocktails or wine afterwards, and would then warm-salt-water the new piercings together when we got back to the flat.

I remember, the Monday after you died, one week later almost to the hour, going to Camden to get a piercing. It was October; it was something we would have done together – had done together, every October, for years. I remember walking down the high street and realising that Eclipse, like you, was gone. I got the piercing anyway, a forward helix, in a basement shop across the road.

I remember 'October Passing', by Melvin Dixon.

I remember Mildreds. Tsunami. Condesa. Wagamama. Wasabi. Lola's.

I remember sushi. I remember vegetarian sushi.

I remember 'there's a fire in the sausage tree', and other poetic and nonsensical drunken mishearings.

I remember telling you about Bob Mortimer's Babybel candle, and the three of us instantly trying to make our own (with mixed success and much smoke).

I remember how you would talk, laugh, and orchestrate what sometimes sounded like high-stakes board meetings, sometimes like torture chambers, in your sleep.

I remember Blue Teddy. I remember Christmas.

I remember 'it's so meaningless to eat' (O'Hara).

I remember, two weeks after you died, a Monday, almost to the hour, going to Brighton to swim in the sea. The weekend had been stormy; there were signs all over the beach warning against swimming. But I swam: partly to try and reach you; partly to feel the sharp, icy drench of the surf and so forget. The sea at Brighton seems to relish its power, like an athlete at the height of their powers, like a young dark cat, like the large brown gulls who soar on the wind. The water is strong, and swiftly deep, and cold, of course, and clear, and the millions of large pebbles that comprise the long sloping beach roil noisily under its surf. Around the groins, two swimmers warned, there have been drownings. I remember that it was difficult to leave the water – the profound, seductive suck, the shifting earth, my sense that you were somewhere in this moving water too, that all seas are connected. The sky was a bright, impossible, Nilgiri blue, I remember, and afterwards we went for sushi.

I remember feeling that my grief was something I could hold. *Had* to hold. That it was unwieldy, unimaginably heavy, fragile, and profoundly precious. That I couldn't put it down.

I remember my whole body ached for weeks after you died – that I even developed a limp. I had not known grief could be so deeply somatic.

I remember how your body often ached, inexplicably: your swollen joints, the taciturn agony of your back.

I remember Sinéad O'Connor, 'Nothing Compares 2 U', and how I had it stuck in my head for weeks after you died, which seemed unfair.

I remember (different register), from *Gossip Girl*: 'Not enough!!'

I remember Taylor Swift. I remember running by the River

Lea, the sibilant reeds towering and vocal, sobbing to a song about August.

I remember Adwaith: another power of three.

I remember Let's Eat Grandma.

I remember First Aid Kit.

I remember Patti Smith.

I remember PUP.

I remember 'the sensation of falling off / the round, turning world' (Bishop).

I remember 'my life held precariously in the seeing hands of others' (O'Hara).

I remember the gifts my friends sent me, after you died. These included:
- flowers (I can't now remember what kind, but they were beautiful)
- a black cashmere sweater
- a turtleneck top, black with pink cats curled up all over it
- a candle, and more flowers
- a copy of C. S. Lewis's *A Grief Observed*
- a copy of Chimamanda Ngozie Adichie's *Notes on Grief*, and a notebook
- a bounty of teas, and a teapot warmer
- a stained glass turtle

- some sea glass, and a silver star, threaded on a chain
- Scotch whisky, 'for days when you need to take the edge off'
- Don Julio tequila (one year later)
- a DryRobe
- a silver charm bracelet – the charm was the letter 'K'
- a knitted woollen blanket
- a book of poems
- a sand dollar.

I remember, after it happened, the first time I dreamed about you. It was such an ordinary dream: a public park, some kind of urban festival, you, us, sitting on grass. How hard it was to wake up.

I remember getting a message from Sophie that read: 'Sabina says they have done the cremation now'.

I remember seeking out cocktails that afternoon, Martin and I: negronis at a bar in Hackney, a grotty place, seemingly nameless, that seemed to have come unstuck in time. It was Halloween. Cocktails were either served in plastic takeaway cups or thick crystal tumblers. The music they played was from our early youth, pop classics by Britney Spears, Ricky Martin, Lou Bega, Weezer, and Atomic Kitten.

I remember Chanel. The red lipstick you bought me (razorblade-free, we joked, unlike in *Killing Eve*) and the waterproof mascara I bought you.

I remember, two days after you died, a Wednesday, going out to buy the most expensive waterproof mascara I could find.

Dior – your favourite.

I remember 'i was ugly with your going' (Danez Smith). I am ugly with your going. Still. But I also know that you taught me that it matters to look good.

I remember Doris Lessing – how her writing somehow helped me through some of the ugliest moments of your going.

I remember your friends. Frankie. Hilda. Steph. Bella. Sofie.

I remember your boyfriend. Solin.

I remember, three days after you died, a Thursday, a Google 'memory': 'four years ago today'. A picture of you – sitting on mum's sofa, wearing your trademark RUN-DMC t-shirt and leggings, holding baby Rudi aloft. I remember that I was at work because work never told me I could go home.

I remember, when baby Larry, nephew number one, was born, and you and I became aunties for the first time, how unbelievable and amazing you and I found it all (I remember thinking, 'like a James Schuyler poem').

I remember how angry you could be. I remember wondering what will happen to all of your fury now that you're dead.

I remember thinking about your dive gear, and wondering about whether or not I could wear it. I remember learning, later, that mum and Sophie had told Sabina that she could give it all away, or keep it. I remember being ok with this. I remember Sabina giving me your dive computer and your fins.

I remember the second dream I had about you, after you died. We three were together; King Kong had been caught and tethered; you stayed with him whilst Sophie and I left to drive into town. How nothing made sense. How hard it was to wake up.

I remember wanting to wear all the clothes I have that you also had. Black leotard. Black Joni jeans from Topshop (Topshop also gone now). Superga shoes. Spike earring. Shark necklace.

I remember climbing Greenwich Hill and thinking about you.

I remember thinking how strange it is to be so completely preoccupied by one person, for so long.

I remember seemingly constant references to death and funerals in films and TV shows. I remember how remote they seemed. This wasn't *your* death. I didn't feel 'triggered'. Triggered instead by walking past Wasabi for the first time after you died. By certain harmonies. By hearing Spanish. By seeing the sea.

I remember, for the longest time – I can't listen to music.

I remember 'was. then wasn't' (Danez Smith).

I remember Grandma telling me that she lost her mum when her mum was just 34. When she was eight.

I remember Aunty Joy lost her baby.

I remember Laura lost her dad.

I remember I lost my sister.

I remember I have a dead sister.

I remember a colleague, whose baby daughter was stillborn, telling a group of us at an unconscious bias training workshop, when asked, that he had 'two children, one deceased'. I remember thinking about the courage and the pain held in those four words. I remember that I have two sisters, one deceased.

I remember Martin saying: 'you'll always be a three'.

I remember little sisters. These include:
- Bella
- Charlotte
- Alison
- Melanie
- Imogen
- Eleanor
- Roisin
- Lucy
- Kizzie
- Hannah
- Sophie
- Fiona
- Mum
- Eloise
- Rowena
- Freya.

I remember big sisters. Me. Dolla. Amy. Yasmine. Laura. Cath.

Joanna. Alice. Fallon. Gerry. Morven.

I remember *Big Sister and Little Sister*.

I remember big sisters and little sisters.

I remember *My Naughty Little Sister*.

I remember big sisters and middle sisters and little sisters.

I remember 'Boots of Spanish Leather'. I remember 'Two Ribbons'.

I remember writing (and giving), in my head, as Martin and I walked by the Bow Back Rivers, the eulogy I wanted for your funeral. I remember that everyone would be encouraged to cry as much and as hard as they wanted to.

I remember 'lost'.

I remember 'bereft'.

I remember 'shattered'.

I remember 'I feel like I've been stabbed'.

I remember understanding what it means to be 'gutted'. Feeling opened up, rent.

I remember 'unbearable'.

I remember 'unmoored'.

I remember 'untethered'.

I remember practically having to beg to reschedule a lecture, just two days after you died.

I remember going to work; I remember working. I remember not really understanding why people told me that it was 'good to keep busy' or 'the distraction will be helpful'. As if I could be 'distracted' from this, from you. I remember: distraction is not comfort, is not comforting.

I remember teaching a seminar on Joe Brainard's *I Remember*. A student commented on the absence of Joe's brothers in his memories of childhood. I remember thinking that when we're children our siblings are so much a part of our existence – our lives, our environments – that we don't really think about them. They're just there. Until suddenly they're not. Like Joe himself. Like you.

I remember 'someone of us are dead / but they are alive in language' (Danez Smith).

I remember, after you died, whenever I pictured you in my head, how weirdly tall you'd become.

I remember that you are there, 5000 miles away, in Santa Catalina, Panama, and that you are not.

I remember Kizzie's little voice, as Sophie told me on the phone that you were dead, asking with curiosity: 'Aunty Kim is dead?'

I remember that it was only her saying that that made me understand.

I remember that Kizzie will never know you. That Rudi, and even Larry, will never know you. The enormity of that loss.

I remember that you will never teach them to dive.

I remember your lion's mane. I remember 'the longest hair in the family' (alternately mine and yours). I remember detangling spray. I remember sea hair. I remember S-Tigi hair oil. I remember how you styled your hair in a way that hid your ears, which you thought stuck out (an inherited anxiety rather than a reality). I remember dad saying: 'your hair is like spun gold'. I remember how mad you used to get when he said it.

I remember your temper. I remember mine. I remember how angry you could make me. I remember a huge fight we had over a desk, in the corridor of the wooden house at Turi. What geeks. I remember how hilarious we found that fight, that desk, for years to come, but how devastating it was on the day it happened.

I remember 'ways to be rich', a list of screwball suggestions that we devised together my first year at university, running to several pages and including 'steal cheese'.

I remember the food parcels you used to send me when I was at university and you were still at school – parcels containing filched mostly non-perishable mini-foods from the school canteen, including packets of jam, KitKats, and the unassailable Babybel.

I remember how you always gave the best gifts. You were an unparalleled gift-giver. Gifts you gave me, and Martin, included:
- our carafe
- the sausage tree (now deceased)
- a small ornamental motorbike from Ibiza
- an Argentinian trick wine holder
- my earring tree
- countless gorgeous bits of jewellery
- my red Chanel lipstick
- the framed black and white watercolor of a tropical bird I haven't been able to identify, that hangs above my desk.

I remember the feeling of 'something awful is about to happen'. I remember that it already has.

I remember Dolly Parton.

I remember Doris Lessing.

I remember Dolla.

I remember: grief is like a mountain. Only no way over, no way round.

I remember that, from cutting myself to running to piercings to tattoos to sex to swimming in very cold water – my body offers a way of coping with my mind.

I remember: high-functioning depressive.

I remember the first dream I had in which I knew you were dead. In the dream, though, you were still alive.

I remember seven geese, standing in a row under a bridge in the Olympic Park, preening their feathers. The sounds of their beaks in the quiet morning light. Then twelve more, swimming in a long thread. Then two more, and then two swans, and then a cormorant coming in to land.

I remember five ducks landing on water, swirling down like autumn leaves on a lightly breezy day.

I remember 'I come into the still presence of water' (Wendell Berry).

I remember that, mostly on Saturdays (though not always), people feed the ducks and geese and swans and coots.

I remember that someone leaves small piles of sunflower hearts on the path by the water in the Olympic Park.

I remember the words of a friend: 'this is catastrophic'.

I remember: something catastrophic has happened to me and no one will acknowledge it.

I remember: not no one.

I remember seeing your Glucagon injection in its orange case on the top shelf of the fridge, a few days after you died. It's still there, in case you need it when you come back.

I remember: it has been five weeks.

I remember: this time yesterday.

I remember: this time one week ago, two weeks, three weeks, four. Five, six, seven. Twenty-four. Thirty.

I remember you and me and Martin sinking four bottles of red wine at The Gun, sitting outside (Covid), using a stick we'd found on the pavement to keep turning the overhead heater on.

I remember going for old fashioneds with Martin on the 33rd floor of the Shard, in your honour. They were good, but made too quickly. Far below, the London Bridge interchange. I remember changing trains there to come visit you when you lived in Croydon.

I remember you asking me for my passport number, in the summer, over Whatsapp. You were in Panama City, staying in a container hotel and applying for residency and a bank account. Some people were having loud sex next door. I was at Trent Bridge, watching the cricket. You needed my passport number because you were listing me as the beneficiary for 30,000 dollars worth of life insurance on your new Panamanian bank account. I replied, sending the number, and saying, I remember, 'please don't die!'. You replied, I remember, 'haha.. might be worth it ☺ Thanks a ton'. I remember, though we never got the money anyway, it's not worth it.

I remember:
    ... *you and I*

Are suddenly what the trees try

To tell us we are:
That their merely being there
Means something   (John Ashbery).

I remember mum saying to me: 'you were such a good big sister to her'.

I remember, you were such a good little sister to me.

I remember the neighbourhoods where you lived in London, and some of the apartments. Whilst we have always been in Bow (following a brief stint first in Limehouse and then in Mile End), you lived in Manor House, Croydon, Whitechapel, and Brixton.

I remember Homerton Hospital. I remember Barts. I remember our terrible GP, and our kind one. I wonder if they know (it turns out they do not).

I am so angry.

I am so sad.

I remember how much we both hated wearing shoes. And clothes for that matter. They 'oppressed our souls'. I remember this was the last thing we ever talked about on Whatsapp.

I remember that all the things people have said to me about you since you died are true.

I remember that I will never see you again. That you will never come back. Never knock on our door, or ring the buzzer, having tailgated your way into the building so stylishly, brown and skinny and absurdly laden with luggage (dive gear and about two hundred bikinis), an exotic creature out of place in grey autumnal London yet always quite at home in our flat.

I remember that you will never have another diabetic seizure on our sofabed (also now deceased). That we will never again come flying down the stairs to coax you back to us, with honey or Lucozade or orange juice or jam or Glucagon. That we will never again, short-sighted (no time to put glasses on) and with fumbling hands, plunge the lifegiving needle into your thigh and then wait wait wait for you to come back to yourself. Never again hold you afterward and comfort you, offer you toast, tea, paracetamol. That this time, if this is what happened, on your own in your hilltop apartment overlooking the Pacific, you didn't recover.

I remember how scary your hypos were, always, even after so long. I remember that no one ever really taught us what to do when you had one. Helping you always felt like winging it, something too important to be winged.

I remember how you hated what having diabetes did to your teeth and to your memory. And how you talked about it, and were sometimes angry.

I remember that your memory was failing.

I remember how you hated the idea that people might think you had Type *Two* diabetes.

I remember how you told everyone that the scar on your shin was from a snake bite.

I remember how little you were when you first started school.

I remember that you won the 'Brain of Turi' prize at the end of your last year there. Eloise reminded me. It was a prize created specially for you, I think, because you had effectively won all of the prizes, but for the sake of the other pupils they couldn't give them all to you. I remember how mad you were to miss out on the riding prize.

I remember how good you were at riding. Little you, flying over jumps, first on sweet Fergie, then on Cloud, dappled grey, fat like a spring, your soulmate, soul delight.

I remember you ringing up school to get my A Level results for me, pretending to be me.

I remember driving fast through a massive puddle, once, and flooding the engine. For some reason you were in jodhpurs and riding boots, and it was a hot, humid day, but you still ran all the way home to get help.

I remember you falling backwards off the water tank where we used to swim – a good ten feet.

I remember Mr Norris, another grey soulmate of yours.

I remember your Siberian dwarf hamsters, and how they multiplied: their sharp teeth, their tiny little pink grubs of babies. How Mr Norris knocked their cage over when we were away at the coast, and ate all of them but one.

I remember you feeding Mr Norris a chipolata and him vomiting it up on your rug. I remember you refusing to clean it up.

I remember how you called Puddock, our gorgeous long-haired Jack Russell named after a solipsistic Scottish toad, only pup and gentlest creature the world has ever known, 'Puddy Buddy'.

I remember our three bantams, Madonna, Caesar, and Mussolini.

I remember our two tortoises, Houdini and Houdini II, both of whom (naturally) escaped.

I remember your little room in the Turi house, with its adjoining door to Sophie's little room.

I remember how you always begged me and Sophie to play tennis with you, or go swimming, and how we never would.

I remember: 'you're such a tart' and other sisterly platitudes.

I remember how stylish you were, and how much I wanted to look more like you.

I remember how much we both loved expensive perfume.

I remember cupcakes (mainly, cupcake icing). I remember angel slices. Dairylea Dunkers (jumbo tubes). Wensleydale with cranberries. Babybels. Reece's Pieces. Tangfastics. Brownies. Soy sauce. Kecap manis. Ketchup. Ham and ketchup. Pasta and ketchup. Cashew nuts.

I remember how mad dad used to get at how much ketchup you used.

I remember when you realised that you *did* like Jessica's homemade chutney after all (a sad day for me because you ate so much of it).

I remember gouda. How the man in the cheese shop in Nakuru would slice a little extra on top of our order, so we could eat it on the drive home.

I remember that you never learned to drive in Kenya.

I remember how much you loved Christmas cake (mainly the icing), especially Mr. Kipling's Christmas slices.

I remember, one Christmas, you and I, very drunk, offering a slice of Christmas cake to the concierge; I remember that he said he wasn't allowed to accept it as he might be accused of drinking on the job.

I remember hearing Clyde McPhatter and the Drifters' version of 'White Christmas' and immediately sharing it with you – that falsetto...

I remember how much you loved Mariah Carey's Christmas song.

I remember how much you loved to cuddle a cat – any cat, but preferably a big soft one like both of ours. I remember how tiny your island pusses always seemed by comparison.

I remember scorpions in your shoes, centipedes down your back, spiders in your ceiling. I remember how much you hated snakes and lizards. How you were stung (at least twice) by a centipede. How you didn't mind spiders – we had long conversations about them – not even the tarantula who lived under your fridge. The big golden orb weaver spider that lived above your house in Costa Rica, the orb weavers that colonised, with their strong yellow silks, the kei apple hedge in our garden in Kenya. The rat that lived in the wall. I remember: 'embrace the rat (not literally)'.

I remember going to the Soho Theatre with you and Martin, Alice and Leigh, to see Angelos Epithemiou. Partway through the show a gigantic rat appeared and began meandering slowly across the floor toward us, before disappearing under our seats. Angelos was funny, but this, I remember from the tears coursing down our faces, was funnier.

I remember Sophie getting a jellyfish's long blue poisonous tentacles wrapped around her ankle on the beach at Vipingo, when we were very little, and you running wildly across the sand to get help.

I remember you falling through a rotted guard rail at the coast, aged about two; you tumbled down a steep, rocky slope, and for weeks had a huge pink scab on your forehead that everyone thought would leave a scar. It didn't.

I remember your cow's lick.

I remember your balayage.

I remember that you and I could talk for hours about sharks: ragged toothed, great white, bull, black tip reef, white tip reef, nurse, oceanic white tip, hammerhead, kitefin, manta... And about octopuses, turtles, nudibranchs, morays, and cuttlefish...

I remember that one year and two months after you died, we finally saw oceanic white tips, at Elphinstone reef, off the coast of Marsa Alam. That dive was for you.

I remember the nurse sharks who watched you teach us to dive; how they seemed to laugh (along with you) as we repeatedly flunked out on the buoyancy test.

I remember 'boy' = buoy. I remember 'booee' = buoy.

I remember introducing you to the music of Mama Cass Elliot (though actually *Lost* did that), to Kirsty MacColl, and to Joan Baez, and how much you liked them.

I remember all of your clothes that became my clothes. I remember that now there are more that will become mine, and I wonder if, how, I will be able to wear them.

I remember the space (not a very big space) your stuff used to take up in our cupboard whilst you were away, and how apologetic you were about it.

I remember the letters – from the bank, from the GP, from the diabetes team at Barts – that used to come here for you whilst you were away. That still come, sometimes. I remember the medication, wrapped in ice packs and sheep wool. I remember the couriers.

I remember our ferocious and funny conversations about how all of our friends were getting married and having babies, and how we, in our different ways, were doing neither.

I remember 'what good is a name / if no one answers back?' (Danez Smith)

I remember your freckles (like mine – though you tanned more easily). I remember your ears (like mine – neither stick out particularly, though we always thought they did).

I remember the time you and Sophie came to the farmhouse near York where I lived during my second and third years at university, and absolutely disgraced yourselves in two different but equally disgraceful ways.

I remember how you and I could both hold our drink (most of the time). I remember how much I appreciated this about you.

I remember Sophie's wedding: how emotional you were as we walked down the aisle together as bridesmaids, literally shuddering with suppressed sobs, and then how you and me and Martin partied until the sun came up. I remember the train ride back to London on the hottest day of the year. Our stinking hangovers, and you saying 'someone please dig me a hole and cover it in...'

I remember weather. Forty-degree days in London; four-inch snow days; floods up to and over Oyster card readers; gusts of wind that rip the roof of the Millennium Dome right off. No you to share them with. No you to hear *'Look!'*, or *'Feel!'*, or *'Imagine!'*

I remember visiting mum and dad, and you being there.

I remember what an incredible aunt you were – Aunt Tim. Deeply silly, wildly generous.

I remember you helping mum foist a gigantic yellow courgette on us.

I remember how much you hated peas, cooked carrots, mushrooms, and baked beans.

I remember that you lived in Nottingham and Manchester before London.

18th October, 2021, a Monday – the worst day of my life. But there have been worse days since, I remember.

I remember reading your death certificate, written in Spanish.

I remember using Google Translate to interpret the documentation relating to your death. The descending chill, the sense of the onset of a frightening hallucination, of seeing those words emerge on my screen.

I remember, in the middle of supper, or when having a shower, or going for a run, bursting into tears.

I remember a new kind of crying.

I remember that you weren't supposed to be there. That it was October, and you should have been here – you were always here in October. That the pandemic, and the 'red list', had kept you there, had meant that everything was scrambled up. I wonder if things could have been different.

I remember that you never got to meet Bella's baby son, Cassian, or Frankie's new daughter, Octavia, or Hilda's baby Maia, all born that same October. That you were supposed to be Cassian's godmother and that Bella never got the chance to ask you.

I remember that those girls have told those babies all about you.

I remember that you never got a chance to admire our beautiful new bathroom and kitchen, or luxuriate in our rainforest shower. The family waterbaby, you would have loved it. I remember Martin saying how sad he felt about that – how he had looked forward to teasing you for using up all the hot water.

I remember that I always feared this day would come. Because of your health, but also because I loved you.

I remember catastrophising – how this catastrophe came true.

I remember how desperately I wanted to get on a plane to come and find you.

I remember how much I didn't want you to have gone through this — dying, being dead — on your own.

I remember David Wojnarowicz contemplating the possibility that David Hujar, in the moments after his death from AIDS, felt 'afraid or confused by his own death'.

I remember 'we remind ourselves repeatedly that our own loss is nothing compared to the loss experienced (or, the even worse thought, not experienced) by he or she who died' (Didion).

I remember: 'at least...'.

I remember: I am not ready for your positive spin on this.

I remember sobbing in train station toilets — Euston, New Street, Marylebone, Moor Street; on trains, on platforms, on the walk to my office, on the walk back from my office, on the walk between the tube and the station, between the tube and home, home and the tube.

I remember that wearing a mask (Covid) conceals the rictus of my crying mouth.

I remember that your last message to us, sent just a few hours before you died, was about a photo that Sophie had shared, of Kizzie sitting on a barstool in a pub (Soph's kids are pub kids).

I remember 'oh fuck fuck fuck fuck fuck'. Whispering. Martin kneeling. And everything going quiet.

I remember your Casio. I remember mine. I remember Sophie's.

I remember 'grief's tyranny is that it robs you of remembering the things that matter' (Adichie). Do I remember the things that matter?

I remember 'acute metabolic disorder' ('Trastorno metabólico agudo').

I remember: I don't really understand what that means.

I remember: how can I not fully understand what that means? How and why you died? Why can I not ask? Why can no one tell me?

I remember the moon, lying on her back.

I remember: I wish I could have protected you.

I remember: I should have protected you.

I want you to come back.

I want for this not to have happened.

I remember: I'm afraid of entering a year not touched by you.

I remember: your birthday is coming up, which I know you hated (*especially* the song). I always loved picking out a present for you, to try and change your mind about birthdays. The aspidistra I bought you last year, which I was never able to give you, is growing strong.

I remember: the sausage tree is not. The sausage tree, which you gave me, is dead.

I remember that I will never see you again.

I remember 'Make Your Own Kind of Music' and how this song could have been written about you.

I remember fighting in the back seat of the car.

I remember 'We're having fun, sittin' in the backseat, huggin' and a-kissin' with Fred – *oh Freddie!*'

I remember how you and Cedric, the youngest girl and the oldest boy, collaboratively lit the sawdust trail in the shape of a phoenix, on Phoenix Night, Turi's version of bonfire night. How tiny you were.

I remember the funny little steampunk man you used to wear as a necklace. How all babies loved it.

I remember how much you always admired and appreciated our flat, and how much that meant to us.

I remember how much I loved cooking for you.

I remember climbing Alfred's Tower with you, and how windy it was; how our long hair blew about madly, Rose Red and Rose White, and how we took the most amazing photo of ourselves, which now I can't find but can still vividly see.

I remember sleeping out under the stars with you, and hearing elephants walking around in the dark nearby. I remember waking at dawn; I remember the tea we drank, wrapped up in our duvets, by the smoking campfire.

I remember our bare feet.

I remember all the times you came to stay.

I remember how we always only nearly-cried when we said goodbye.

I remember: 'You think that you have time. And then, all at once, you don't' (Jessie Greengrass).

I remember long walks by the canal, talking with you on the phone, thousands of miles away, wherever you happened to be.

I remember our Whatsapp chats. How they're still there. How I can't bear, now, to read them. How you 'left' our group chats.

I remember recommending Fiona Apple to you, and how diplomatically you confessed you didn't like her.

I remember recommending The Skints to you, and how good it felt when you said you liked them too.

I remember how much you liked reggae.

I remember how much you liked terrible commercial electro.

I remember how pale you liked your tea.

I remember people visiting us, and not saying a word about what had happened.

I remember the friends who didn't get in touch. I remember the friends who did.

I remember my mind diverging into two parallel tracks. On the one track, the one that people see, I am quite normal, can function, talk, laugh often. On the other, everything is shrouded in darkness, and I am screaming with pain, with fury.

I remember: what happened to all your earrings?

I remember that I have one (actually I have many) – a silver ray, one half of a pair that you sent me along with a little note that reads, 'Not a Christmas present – just because you're rather lovely, that's all!'.

I remember that your handwriting never grew up.

I remember you not being able to reproduce your own signature at a crucial juncture in your application for Panamanian residency.

I remember: a man called Ollie has brought all your 'valuables' back to the UK. I don't know what your valuables consist of.

I remember: Sophie and I will travel to Panama to scatter your ashes on the water where you dived. I can hardly comprehend, let alone say, the words 'your ashes'.

I remember I'm not sure how to get from Panama City to Santa Catalina. I think: I'll ask Kim. Then I remember.

I remember drinking Toñas in various beachside bars in Little Corn, Nicaragua, with you and Martin and assorted street puppies and cats and chickens.

I remember how you killed the little lime tree I gave you by drowning it in washing up liquid in a misguided attempt to rid it of bugs.

I remember that Martin and I planted trees for everyone's Christmas presents in the jungle on Kalimantan. I wonder how tall yours is now, if it survived.

I remember how you used to bite your cheeks when someone took a photo of you.

I remember Amy apologizing, after meeting up with me for the first time since you died, if she had used any 'clumsy words' (she hadn't).

I remember that seeing friends, and talking about you, and talking about losing you, is at once therapeutic and, especially afterwards, unbearably difficult.

I remember you always sent me a birthday present (sometimes more than one), even when you were thousands of miles away.

I remember that you and one of your friends came to the creative writing club that Jess and I set up at school.

I remember getting the plane back home with you, and back to school: how scared I was that you would have a hypo (which you sometimes did), and how funny your sleeptalking could be.

I remember Cairo airport, and the day we spent there, when our connecting flight home was cancelled. Trying to explain to airport staff about your diabetes, when you refused to say anything. How we had nothing to eat until a strange sandwich and a Fanta, I think, materialised in some kind person's hands. The plastic bucket seats.

I remember you buying your various (increasingly thick) wetsuits, and trying them on in the incongruously non-nautical space of mum's carpeted bathroom in Somerset.

I remember how much you loved London, just like Martin and me.

I remember walking past Aidan Turner (aka Mitchell the vampire from *Being Human*) on the road outside our flat and instantly wanting to tell you about it; I remember passing him outside Mile End Cemetery and wondering, with Martin, if he was going there to feed.

I remember thinking how much you would have appreciated the sight of two car-sized silver baubles, broken free from their moorings thanks to a storm called 'Claudio', bowling dumbly down an autumnal Tottenham Court Road.

I remember wanting to tell you about the man from Telford who was caught stealing 200,000 Creme Eggs.

I remember that you had 20:20 vision – the only one out of all of us.

I remember that we called you 'the family hippo' due to the state you left mum's bathroom in after a shower.

I remember that you were the family waterbaby.

I remember that you were looking forward to some time off at the end of October.

I remember that I couldn't – still can't, really – look at photos of you. How mum kept sending them and how I couldn't bear to look.

I remember painting our toenails together, on the sofa, in Bow.

I remember you wearing my slippers.

I remember your gorgeous black silk dressing gown – the weighty hang of it, its sexy swish. I remember that I wore it for the first time yesterday.

I remember how long you took in the shower.

I remember 'my sisters'. And 'my sister' – used interchangeably to refer to either of you. I remember 'Rona and her sisters'. I remember 'siste'. I remember 'Bimble'.

I remember: you are not 'in' the things around me. You are not in the sky. You are not 'looking down'. You are not 'in' the magpies on my windowsill. Not in the sea. You are nowhere.

You are gone.

I remember 'The Mystery of the Mystery' (Dolly Parton).

I remember walking down Broad Street in the rain, sobbing underneath my mask.

I remember 'are you ok?' I remember: 'yes'. I remember: 'how are you doing?' I remember: 'ok'. I remember: 'you're doing amazingly'. I am none of these things.

I remember: I don't really recognize the version of myself that is simply continuing.

I remember: I can be in two mental spaces at once, teaching poetry whilst also thinking about you.

I remember playing 'Boricua en la Luna' in a seminar and barely holding it together.

I remember how dramatically and uncontrollably your legs used to shake when you drove a car (adrenaline).

I remember that you once took moped lessons in London.

I remember that you had a boat captain's licence.

I remember all the places you lived: Utila, Western Australia, the Cook Islands, Little Corn, Buenos Aires, Costa Rica, Panama.

I remember that you lived in Argentina for a while, with a

lovely Colombian girl who worked with you at Albert&Pearl. I can't remember her name and I wonder if she knows you are dead.

I remember that her name is Carolina. One year and four months after your death, she contacts me. She has just found out.

I remember your incredible marinades.

I remember your brownies.

I remember Martin crying when we watched *Babyteeth*, six weeks after you died, when the sixteen-year-old girl protagonist with the amazing wigs dies from cancer in her sleep. I remember that he woke up around 5am the next morning and couldn't get back to sleep for feeling sad. I remember that Cousin snuggled in between us, as if he knew.

I remember that no matter how cold it got you always went running in a singlet.

I remember us talking about running and looking. You starting to notice things and to take pleasure in them – cows in the field, birdsong, newly-blooming plants – the way I did. I remember the picture of the white cow you sent me.

I remember us sharing memes, as well as photos of cats and other animals. The last one you sent me was of Leonardo DiCaprio in *The Great Gatsby* (a rare Leo film I haven't seen – I don't think you had either) holding up a glass of champagne and saying 'Cheers to the people who love us, the losers who lost us, and the lucky bastards who get to meet us'.

I remember: I feel very far away from my parents in this catastrophe.

I remember the 200 metre swim Martin and I had to do to qualify for our Advanced Open Water license – you, sitting on the boat watching us floundering in the swell, laughing.

I remember night diving with you – the otherworldly bioluminescence that surrounded us, as if we were in the depths of the Milky Way or *A Midsummer Night's Dream* come to life. I remember our terrible underwater torches, the permeable darkness, and the ancient turtle who swam startled from under her rock straight into your arms.

I remember you standing on the jetty at Little Corn, wearing flipflops, waving, as our ferry from the main island pulled in, and we, soaking wet from the surf, scrambled ashore to meet you.

I remember mandazis – both the Kenyan kind and the Little Corn kind.

I remember how Cousin and Lady liked to thoroughly investigate all your luggage whenever you came to stay with us, both before and after going away. I remember taking a bag that had belonged to you to work, a year after, and Lady actually climbing right inside it.

I remember: this time six weeks ago, my sister was alive.

I remember the time we got so drunk at Turi club that I fell in an actual ditch on the way home, and you fell flat on your actual face through the side door of the house when we got home.

I remember coming across an article about the sighting of a 'mythic white sperm whale in Jamaica'. My first impulse was to share it with you. I remember that I can't. I remember how much I miss talking about the ocean with you.

I remember articles about cuttle fish, stingrays, elephant seals. A book called *My Life in Sea Creatures*.

I remember that it's December, and that you won't have a birthday this month. We turn the page on the calendar, and there it is, in the square marking December 30th: 'Kim's bday'.

I remember ginger and lemon tea at Mildreds in Camden, after a piercing, and after gyoza.

I remember how much of our relationship revolved around food and drink.

I remember how much you and I loved talking about food – halloumi, avocados, nasi goreng... how much we loved to eat together ... how much I loved to cook for you ... Or, even better, how much I loved Martin to cook for all three of us, while you and I caught up over a bottle of red wine.

I remember: 'your place is empty' (Kaveh Akbar).

I remember you telling me about the time you and Sophie got

so drunk in Nottingham that she tried to kill you with a bottle of ketchup.

I remember how much you loathed our worm farm: I remember how much I loved telling you to say hello to your 'worm nieces and nephews'.

I remember how the words 'online memorial' derailed me. I still can't think of you as someone who exists in the past tense, as someone who needs to be remembered, online.

I remember closing your accounts: banks, social media, emails, and more. The digital footprints of a life.

I remember hives. I remember nausea. I remember losing three kilos in six weeks without even trying. I remember tinnitus. Vertigo. Disordered eating.

I remember that 'my sister', that magically deictic term, has now become literal. 'My sister' now just means Sophie. I have one, where once I had two.

I remember you and your Austrian dive instructor friend Sofie, who was beautifully, extravagantly tattooed, coming to listen to me give a talk at the LSE about women poet-editors in 1960s New York. You were both so gorgeous and vibrant and attentive, and wonderfully at odds with that dingy, white-lighted, academic room on the lower ground floor of the library. We went for drinks, afterward, at the Ship, in Holborn, with Martin.

I remember you telling me about Sofie's bird house outside

her flat near Vienna, and asking for bird-attracting tips to share with her.

I remember Sofie coming over for dinner. I remember that Sofie's bird house had attracted all the birds, including a vast pigeon, and that she had noticed that their numbers always swelled in the days before a cold snap, as they fattened themselves up for warmth.

I remember giving Sofie your whale-tail necklace.

I remember you and me eating sushi at a restaurant on Kingsway and nearly suffocating because the pieces were so huge (*not* a first-date restaurant!).

I remember sake at Tsunami.

I remember how much you loved nasi goreng.

I remember trying to get you to watch *Queer Eye* and *Ru Paul's Drag Race* in the hope you that you might learn to love yourself a bit more.

I remember that you thought that no one really loved you; I wish you could know how much that wasn't – isn't – true.

I remember wondering if you knew I was queer.

I remember *Pet Sematary*.

I remember *The Dark Half.*

I remember that I will always associate the Spanish language and documentaries about the ocean with you. Are there trigger warnings for these?

I remember the time you returned to Santa Catalina to find one of your little cats lying dead in the grass near your house. I remember wanting to give you the tightest hug. How hard and sad that day and those that followed must have been.

I remember your stories about the things you had seen and done and heard underwater – the creatures, the adventures, the clients.

I remember you being attacked by ferocious hybrid bees when you stopped for lunch on a remote island in Coiba National Park – an island that was little more than a sandbar. How you all fled, diving under the water to escape, and how the bees followed, and waited for you on the surface, even following the boat in mad pursuit. I remember the great horn-like sting on your forehead.

I remember long conversations with you on Whatsapp video, in the early days of the pandemic, when you would show me around where you lived, in your bikini, shorts, and flipflops. Your blue bungalow, your hammock, your beach, your creek, your ocean (at that time oddly out of bounds).

I remember that Panama instigated a gendered curfew during the early days and weeks of the pandemic.

I remember thinking: you shouldn't come back to England. You'll hate it here.

I remember that the last year and a half of your life was pretty miserable.

I remember wishing you weren't so lonely.

I remember that you will never see the new episodes of *La Casa de Papel* and *Into the Night*, and that I'll never be able to talk about them with you. I remember you saying that you didn't want to watch the new season of *La Casa de Papel* until Solin was able to watch it too – and wondering, as we watched it, if we should be waiting for you too.

I remember how much you would have liked *Yellowjackets*, and how much we would have liked talking about it.

I remember that you'll never ring me up to tell me about the latest ridiculous thing you've done in your sleep.

I remember that you'll never get your second, or third, Covid jab.

I remember the kindness of some of my students, to whom I'd obliquely (by necessity) indicated your loss. Kate, who acknowledged in writing how hard it must be to be at work; George, who repeatedly offered to postpone our meetings and who always asks how I'm doing; Phoebe, who included a content warning in an email in which she mentioned her own sister.

I remember thinking, having thrown up before dinner one Tuesday, 'I have grief', as if it were some kind of disease. I remember the character of Tayo, in Leslie Marmon Silko's

Ceremony, bedridden with nausea upon his return from war. I remember 'the disease of despair'.

I remember 'the mourner is in fact ill' (Melanie Klein).

I remember the time a bird pooped on Sophie's head at Bristol Temple Meads station and how you and I could *not stop laughing*.

I remember how profoundly silly you could be.

I remember drinking rosé with you and Martin on a hot summer's day, a Friday, in the Park East gardens, surrounded by drama as one of the ground floor flats had caught fire and everyone had turned out to watch.

I remember introducing you to our lovely Geordie neighbour, Ange.

I remember you meeting Bina.

I remember that you knew Katie, who looks after our cats.

I remember that I haven't been able to tell any of them that you are dead. When I speak to them, it's in a parallel world in which you still exist.

I remember that you died just two weeks after Katie's beloved cat Maj, or Uncle Maj, who was sixteen and had grown very thin.

I remember that we were going to spend Christmas together,

but that 'Tier 4' regulations ruined our plans at the very last minute, and so you had to spend it alone.

I remember that you were going to stay at Jess's house in Brockley, to look after her cat Riley, and that we were planning a surprise birthday picnic for you in Greenwich Park, with champagne, sushi, and cake. That didn't happen either. I remember that you spent your last birthday alone. I remember that I bought you an aspidistra and some Chanel mascara, which didn't arrive in time.

I remember someone sending you the weirdest birthday card (some kind of boomer joke about social media, which you didn't really use) and how neither of us could understand it and how hilarious we found the whole thing.

I remember hair mascara.

I remember how you said you always struggled to put mascara and eyeliner on (always looked pretty great to me).

I remember you never went anywhere or did anything without makeup on – even coming up after a dive, on a boat in the Pacific in a howling gale, you'd reapply.

I remember the Christmas photo of you, me, and Martin, with the red wine in the carafe. I remember what a Christmas that was, even though I don't remember most of it.

I remember the mice in your Whitechapel flat, and how it looked onto the tracks at Whitechapel station.

I remember the times you stayed on our sofa while you looked for a room to rent in London. I remember house-hunting with you – even going with you one time to some phony 'interview' with a bunch of stuck-up creepy girls in a house in Plaistow. I remember one flat in Poplar where the tenants offered you tea, and you said no, and later I said that you should have said yes, so that they would think you were sociable or something, and you started crying as we walked down Fairfield Road. Actually, I loved your unsociability – because it was real, and because you were true to it, and because I feel it too, and because I am not.

I remember the boys you dated. 'Bad characters', rarely good to you, or not for long; usually handsome. I remember wishing you would find someone who would be as good to you as Martin is to me.

I remember the tiffs you and Martin used to have. How easily he could make you cry. But also how much and how easily he could make you laugh.

I remember that the grief I feel – this feeling of no longer knowing my own body, my own mind – is a tribute to the enormity of the space you occupied in my life, that you still occupy.

I remember Martin telling me that his editor had told him, without specifying the source of his own grief, 'you won't feel right for at least a year'.

I remember you coming with us to a football match (York v. Carlisle) when we were at university. The weather was freezing and Martin was on the verge of coming down with mumps.

I remember remembering the York v. Carlisle match at an Irons v. Brighton match at the Olympic Stadium.

I remember World Cups – how you never got into them, until, like me, you did.

I remember that we did most of our growing up thousands of miles away from home, the three of us, and how crucial we were to each other's lives as a result.

I remember: you are context. You are memories. Memory.

I remember: grief shifts our relationship with time.

I remember: the image of my future has been disrupted (I remember: your future is over).

I remember that my relationship with my past has been altered.

I remember getting the tube with you.

I remember paying you a pound to do the washing up one summer's day at granny's house in Birmingham; granny got really mad at me (and Sophie, who had also paid you a pound to wash up) because she thought we were exploiting you. She didn't realise that it had been your idea, and that you were, as the saying goes, laughing all the way to the bank.

I remember how quick you were at cross-country running –

your knock-kneed little legs speeding up Turi hill or down the red earth tracks of Greenacres.

I remember that in April it will be a year since I saw you for the last time. Then two.

I remember that I am the last person in our family to see you alive.

I remember Martin offering to organise your memorial.

I remember that all your friends are so far-flung that a memorial would be impossible.

I remember that all the physical symptoms of grief – the nausea, headaches, body aches, insomnia, tinnitus – are merely a distraction from the yawning psychic anguish that losing you has caused.

I remember reading, at the beginning of *The Grass is Singing*, that Mary Turner's body was covered with a sheet, and wondering if someone covered you up too. Is it because bodies, death, are somehow shameful? Or simply too much to see?

I remember the first body I ever saw. A man, hit by a car, lying in the middle of the Nakuru highway, at the junction which led to our house.

I remember thinking of you as somehow conscious, as they took your body away to Santiago from Santa Catalina. Do you remember the ride?

I remember mum saying she never expected you to have a long life. I never expected you to have as short a life as this.

I remember someone saying 'she's free of her diabetes'.

I remember thinking: 'she's not free, she's fucking dead'.

I remember someone else saying: 'at least she loved her job and being in the sea with all the sharks'.

I remember thinking: I am happy and love my job but I don't want to be dead.

I remember a colleague and friend spending almost an entire afternoon in my office, ostensibly just shooting the shit, but obviously to look out for or look after me, without actually ever mentioning what had happened.

I remember another colleague knocking on my door, on numerous separate occasions, 'just being neighbourly'.

I remember walking with a colleague and friend in the Winterbourne gardens, talking about you for the first time; talking too about his beloved mum, dead from Covid, also thousands of miles away, and his dad, years ago, dead of an aneurysm in his forties, when my friend was only twenty.

I remember my head of department saying absolutely nothing.

I remember a card from a friend, in which he described you as his 'hero'.

I remember a card from one of my best friends' parents.

I remember Arran whisky from Joanna and Ben.

I remember that you hated to eat in public just as much as I did (especially bananas).

I remember mum always offering you a banana on car journeys, and you always refusing, and getting so mad.

I remember banana and sugar sandwiches.

I remember banana bread.

I remember that you only liked peanut butter in things, not on things (in smoothies, but never on toast).

I remember your tiny denim shorts.

I remember your sunglasses – how we talked about how they didn't have those annoying nose clips that get caught in your hair. How I should get a pair. Now I'm wearing them.

I remember that of everything I remember, there is so much I am forgetting.

I remember your cowboy boots.

I remember when we got our Irish passports.

I remember 'grief is the price we pay for love'.

I remember 'Little sister, the sky is falling' (Patti Smith).

I remember I was expected to be back at work, teaching, just two days after you died. How little understanding there was of just how catastrophic your loss is to me.

I remember how much you loved sweet potatoes.

I remember how much I miss talking about tv shows with you.

I remember that Joanna, Jess, and Ben sent me and Martin a mini Christmas tree – for 'Christmas cheer'.

I remember 'recuperative funds' and a 'Lucky Cat' card, from four beautiful souls at work.

I remember an energised, furious conversation with a friend and colleague at the top of the fourth-floor staircase in the Arts Building.

I remember that everything now is 'before' or 'after'. 'Before' feels somehow sunny, bathed in a kind of light that looks and feels like summer (perhaps because it, literally, was). 'After' is dark, cold, the sky low, no matter how many real summers pass.

I remember that you have friends and former lovers all over the world, some of whose names I don't even know. The friend you lived with in Argentina. The boyfriend from New Zealand. The skyscraper window cleaner and firefighter from Colorado. I wonder if they know. I wonder how I could contact them. I wonder if I should.

I remember how much you preferred the company of men to women.

I remember how much you hated travelling by car, especially in England, where all the windows remain closed.

I remember when you went all the way to Chiswick for a balayage. I remember that you inspired me to get a balayage of my own.

I remember that I entirely re-curated my piercings after you died, in your honour. That it feels kind of pointless because I can't show you.

I remember how you would always hog the fire, no matter whose house we were in.

I remember the most beautiful sunrises, seen through the train window on my journeys to work.

I remember how protective of you I feel when anyone talks about you – how much their easy use of the past tense in reference to you bothers me.

I remember listening to 'Octopus's Garden', walking up Serpentine Road in a light wintry mist-rain, and imagining you there, in the octopus's garden, a little like how O'Hara was imagined by Allen Ginsberg, after his death, as being at a 'garden party in the clouds'.

I remember my colleague and friend bringing me cake, impromptu, one Thursday afternoon; how he shows he cares through the provision of baked goods.

I remember friends checking in with me.

I remember how different it felt teaching the poetry of the AIDS crisis now that I know what it feels like to be bereaved – to be bereft; now that I know grief, know the art of losing; now that a crucial connection to my past and my future has been irrevocably severed; now that every day is a process of navigating memory, navigating the relationship between death and life, navigating the ethics of survival.

I remember: I am haunted.

I remember: ghosts are real, but not in the way we think.

I remember: 'the rain is full of ghosts tonight' (Edna St. Vincent Millay).

I remember 'Mama You've Been On My Mind'.

I remember that your favourite Beatles songs were 'Sexy Sadie' and 'Happiness is a Warm Gun'.

I remember thinking I'll never know what you would have looked like old, or middle aged – that I'll never get to be a disreputable aunty with you, wearing too much perfume, drinking too much wine, swearing in front of the kids.

I remember 'Boy, you're gonna carry that weight a long time'.

I remember mum showing me the photo of you and Larry

that she keeps with your birth certificate – when one brings her down, the other one brings her up. I remember her voice breaking a little as she said this.

I remember 'when someone dies it leaves a hole. It's always in the middle of people'.

I remember 'Rona's so tough'. I don't know why people say that.

I remember that you died alone. That no one was there to tell you everything was ok, to hold your hand. To hold you.

I remember 'grief is necessary. You have to be able to mourn' (Rebecca Brown).

I remember 'How do I recognize this already? Why does all this feel so much like remembering?' (Richard Powers).

I remember going to an Indonesian restaurant off Charing Cross Road with you, Leigh, Alice, and Martin.

I remember cocktails on the house at the St. Martin's Lane Hotel.

I remember: 'she wants only peace. But this is where she lives now'.

I remember: I want to plant a tree.

I remember David Sedaris: 'A person expects his parents to die. But a sibling? I felt I'd lost the identity I'd enjoyed since 1968.'

I remember 'clasping an amulet of words to keep / The leaning dark away' (Hazel Hall).

I remember you getting really drunk at a wedding and being scooped aloft and carried to the car by a 'knight in shining armour'; I remember dad joking about how you stripped the paint off the side of the car when you hung your drunken head out the window to vomit on the drive home.

I remember trips to Lake Bogoria: the long, hot drive, the country music, the chevda and Cokes, the big pool, the hot pool, the hot sun, the stuffed lion in the defunct hotel lobby, the bread-stealing monkeys, the baby bat that fell in the pool and bit my hand when I fished her out, the bee stings, the cats, the goats, the tortoises, the marabou storks, the inevitable overheating of the car radiator on the way home, the sunburns, the calamine lotion.

I remember camping in Nakuru Park: writing and singing 'Ten Bob for the Lion', and the baboons that drank all our squash during the night.

I remember – did you die of a heart attack? Did our Scottish grandfather? Might I?

I remember you and me and Bella getting really into *What Lies Beneath* when we lived at the Menengai house, and how much it always made us scream, no matter how often we watched it.

I remember how much you loved raw dough, which you used

to steal when Esther was making pastry, and raw cake mix.

I remember that you really loved cashews – especially honey roasted.

I remember you eating handfuls of unsalted cashews out of a Tupperware we kept in the second drawer down in the old kitchen.

I remember stopping at the petrol station to buy 'iron rations' on our way back to school on Sundays; and keeping up the tradition by sending 'iron rations' to your various faraway homes over the years.

I remember that you were a really good hockey player.

I remember you recommending *Mission Blue*, the documentary about Sylvia Earle; how brilliant Earle is, and the film.

I remember that the last time I went to get my hair done, you were alive, and I sent you and Sophie a dumb selfie, to our 'LRKlets' Whatsapp group – one of the groups which you have now, somehow, inexplicably, 'left'.

I remember nobody told me you could die from this. Ever.

I remember Dextrose tablets, or 'energy sweets'. How they went from being mountaineering treats dished out by dad whenever we got 'over the brow of the next hill' to being lifesaving quasi-medication for you.

I remember the gigantic Lucozade bottle we bought for you ahead of your visit last Christmas. Which never happened, and which you never used.

I remember not sleeping whenever you stayed with us, too afraid of you having a seizure and neither me or Martin waking up. Turns out Martin wasn't sleeping either.

I remember Martin suggesting I get a tattoo of your furious face on my back. Or hand!

I remember accidentally buying *all* the Amarula in an effort to send you a bottle that last Christmas. Four bottles later, I think you finally got one (meanwhile, Martin drank all the rest).

I remember how much you wanted the cat that lived across the road from you to love you.

I remember the super-tight hood on your new wetsuit that nearly induced a panic attack whenever you tried to put it on.

I remember your freediving fins – and how we used them to enact a 'socially-distanced' hug in King's Cross when you finally got back from Panama in May 2020.

I remember how much you loved freediving, and my and Martin's lame attempts at it in Amed, under the shadow of Gunung Agung.

I remember you using a lighter to permanently de-fog my mask. I remember your advice – you can borrow all your dive gear, but you've got to have your own mask.

I remember all your recommendations for dive gear – fins, masks, booties, dive hooks, dive pointy-things whose name I can't remember.

I remember how much we all wanted to try the underwater dive scooters they used to have in the Red Sea.

I remember the time in Little Corn when the three of us were character-assassinating an arrogant, all-the-gear-and-no-idea Swiss diver who you'd been teaching, only to realise he was sitting right behind us and had heard every word.

I remember the giant crabs and brutal, toe-shattering rocks in the undergrowth on Little Corn.

I remember thinking that I won't ever hear your voice again. I don't have any recordings of you speaking. I remember that I have no voicemails from you, because we're millennials and who leaves voicemails? I remember that you had no answerphone message, because, again, who leaves voicemails? And because you were shy, I have no videos of you either. I wish I could hear your voice. I remember that sometimes I think I do.

I remember having lunch with Sophie, and talking about how fucked up this is: the disordered nature of what has happened. The shock, the disorientation. How we're in our thirties and this isn't supposed to happen.

I remember laughing about how you and I used to wind Sophie up on car journeys – making her sit in the middle and called her Renfield, after the character in *Dracula*.

I remember laughing when she told me that you used to tell her off for calling prosecco 'proshecco'.

I remember, on the train home from that lunch, thinking about the poem or poems I might read when we scatter your ashes. 'I Sing the Body Electric', maybe; or 'Buried at Springs', by Schuyler. 'Our little life is rounded with a sleep', from *The Tempest*. 'At Step Away from Them'. Joyce Grenfell, 'By Herself and her Friends':

> *If I should go before the rest of you*
> *Break not a flower nor inscribe a stone,*
> *Nor when I'm gone speak in a Sunday voice*
> *But be the usual selves that I have known.*
> *Weep if you must – parting is hell.*
> *But life goes on, so sing as well.*

I remember 'Some Trees'. And 'At North Farm'. 'The New Spirit'. 'A Sermon'.

I remember 'Animals' by O'Hara: 'I wouldn't want to be faster / or greener than now if you were with me O you / were the best of all my days'.

I remember, drunk, listening to Kirsty MacColl, 'He's on the Beach', and Martin saying he wanted me to play that song at his funeral. And me saying no, because I was going to die first. And us agreeing to die together.

I remember Sophie saying that she told Kizzie she was going to have lunch with Aunty Rona, and Kizzie asking, 'did she die too?'

I remember Sophie telling me that Larry had said to her: 'Mummy, Kim will be in your heart forever'.

I remember Sophie talking about being stoic, about how she hasn't really cried. But, also, how she feels disoriented, shocked, and literally tingling with anxiety.

I remember talking about CBD, CBT, counselling, beta blockers, diazepam, alcohol, weight loss, headaches, nausea, tingling feet and faces, panic attacks, sweaty palms, and feeling insignificant.

I remember telling Sophie: you are not insignificant to me.

I remember Sophie telling me that mum couldn't look at the photo of your urn, and that she didn't want to see photos of where we will scatter your ashes.

I remember Sophie saying she had asked Sabina to send Solin a hug from us.

I remember I need to learn how planes work, so that I can counsel us both out of our anxiety on the journey to Panama.

I remember that I love running through Pigeon's estate for the cherry trees, and the flock of pigeons, the occasional cat, and the great tits; down Ruston Street for the ivy that flows over the wall, and the tree roots that seam the pavement, and the sparrows.

I remember a dream about you – it was Christmas, and you

were working in a bar, and we invited you over for Christmas day.

I remember another dream (same night): Sophie was getting married, and someone had died, and you and I walked down the aisle behind her, in the Crypt at St Paul's, holding each other close, with people staring at us.

On waking, it took me about half an hour to remember both dreams, and then to remember.

I remember wondering, after seeing a cycle-by mugger try to steal a woman's phone right out of her hands, mid-phone call, one night outside the Bow Bells, what would happen to our messages if I lost my phone.

Martin's birthday. I remember that this is the first time since we met that he didn't get a card from you.

I remember how much you loved *Fargo*, and how this time last year, because you couldn't come to London for Christmas, you and I had some exceedingly detailed conversations about Billy Bob Thornton.

I remember how much you would have liked *Goliath*.

I remember how much I loved our really long chats. I remember how the hours flowed by, mainly in laughter, sometimes in tears, frustration, anger. I wish I could call you this Christmas, not because it's Christmas but because it has now been nine and a half weeks since we spoke.

I remember: 'which way do we / face to talk to the dead? ... Are the dead there / if we do not speak to them?' (Sharon Olds).

I remember Sophie saying that she felt sad watching *Moana* – how a little girl sings about the ocean being her friend and going with it wherever it wants to take her.

I remember being sent a beautiful oceanic trinket, to let me know I was thought of – two ocean pebbles and a silver starfish, linked by a silver chain. A charm that links you with the two who sent it.

I remember: 'She knows she'll never see him again in this or any life to come. Yet she sees him wherever she looks' (Richard Powers).

I remember: 'And all the people who will, in time, turn into other things' (Richard Powers).

I remember not recognizing, or accepting, the language of grief therapy – how 'well' you're 'processing it', etc. As if I'm eating your death, or my grief, or moving through levels of a computer game or learning a language; as if there is somehow a right or a successful way to react when your little sister just doesn't wake up one morning, five thousand miles away. I remember thinking – what are you congratulating me for? For not being dead too? For my performance of survival? For not telling you in intimate and harrowing detail how I really am feeling? You don't want to know.

I remember 'other people don't know what to do with your shit, with the reality of other people's feelings' (Brandon Taylor).

I remember reading an article about boarding schools: 'I remember the feeling of desolate homesickness: abruptly, several times a year, our attachments to home and family were broken. We lost everything – parents, pets, toys, younger siblings...' (Richard Beard). I remember that this is why I feel so close to my sisters – because our relationship was contingent, but also because they ultimately came with me.

I keep remembering that it's nearly your birthday.

Even though we never went in the end, for your birthday, Greenwich Hill somehow reminds me of you – so we'll go there on your birthday this year, with some flowers, some music, some sushi, and some form of delicious cocktail, and celebrate you. I remember that birthdays are a way to celebrate, to *fete*, the people we love, just for being born.

I remember: it is inconceivable to me that you are dead.

I remember that this is forever. It's not so much that you've gone; it's that you're not coming back.

I remember *Grief*, by Andrew Holleran; *Gifts of the Body*, by Rebecca Brown; *The Year of Magical Thinking*, by Joan Didion; *Smash Cut*, by Brad Gooch.

I remember that Joan Didion is dead now too.

I remember: 'it's a day like any other' (Schuyler).

I remember: 'it will become something that happened in another year' (Didion).

I remember: 'Grief was passive. Grief happened. Mourning, the act of dealing with grief, required attention' (Didion). Today is your birthday. Today I am giving my grief my attention by swimming in six-degree wild water.

I remember the cormorant who stood with her wings spread, on a float in the pond, as I swam near and watched.

I remember the women of the pond.

I remember the dogs of the Heath (Shadow).

I remember the sycamore at the top of the hill in Greenwich Park, at the foot of which we laid the flowers we'd brought for you (astroemeria, madiba, solidago, and greenbell). A crow landed on one of the lower branches, consecrating it. Later, two magpies stopped by for cupcake crumbs, in the gathering dark.

I remember the birthday ceremony Martin and I held for you, under the sycamore, overlooking London in her subdued, grand, winter glory. Champagne and poetry – 'Animals', by Frank O'Hara. Sushi and a song – 'Make Your Own Kind of Music' by Cass Elliot. Passionfruit and vanilla cupcakes and cocktails out of cans – an old fashioned and a negroni (each). The wind was fierce but the weather was warm – we attributed both to you. There were fat squirrels in the trees, and a robin, and dogs going up and down the hill.

I remember the darkness of the park as we descended, thoughts of sleeping birds and animals.

I remember the gay pub we sat in afterwards, where we shared a bottle of sauvignon blanc. The sparkling lights, the 1980s and 1990s hit parade on the TV above our heads. And the vegetarian Indian restaurant, where the waitress joined us in mocking the overpriced sock shop opposite.

I remember that we walked through the Greenwich foot tunnel to Island Gardens, where we stopped and looked back across the water at the Cutty Sark, whose sails had been transformed into a gigantic Christmas tree.

I remember our gin and tonic outside the Bow Bells. How a TFL worker had a puncture right there, and how he changed the tyre himself.

I remember that we made plans to go diving in Egypt in February – in the Red Sea, where you always wanted to go and spend time freediving.

I remember that we talked about your ashes – how we've never seen ashes before, how I want to bring some home to Bow.

I remember that I've ordered a rambling rose root that I'm going to plant in the garden for you.

I remember that Cousin Alarm Clock woke us up extra early on your birthday – in tribute to how he always riled you up when you stayed at ours and he did the same thing to you.

I remember 'the difference between grief as we imagine it and grief as it is' (Didion).

I remember 'the void, the very opposite of meaning' (Didion).

I remember: I don't think you'd be too happy about being suddenly dead at the age of 32. I think you'd be really fucking pissed off.

I remember: 'I wake and feel the fell of dark, not day' (Hopkins).

I remember, every year I will visit your sycamore in Greenwich and lay flowers.

I remember that New Years are not really about new beginnings. Tomorrow is just a day like any other. I wonder what fresh horrors this new year will bring.

I remember: memories don't soothe or offer solace when the person with whom you shared them is dead.

I remember wondering why I am able to talk about you so calmly. Is it because I have not stopped thinking about you, about 'it', since 'it' happened? But I still can't say, can't describe, how (why) you died, what happened. I wonder what people think happened to you. I wonder what did.

I remember the glancing pain of the cold water in the Ladies' Pond – the intensity, the shooting sensations in my hands and collarbones. I remember the deep, steady breathing, the enveloping, tranquilising embrace of the dark water, the grey of the winter sky above me when I turn on my back, the blackness of the bare trees, the livingness of the bodies of the women dotted about in the water around me.

I remember that the water at the docks is dark and glassy. Great black iron cranes line the north and south water banks – relics of industry. Planes roar right overhead as they slant down into the nearby airport; the cable car cranks its quiet, airborne furrow to and fro across the river. Four young swans slip back and forth across the swim paths marked out by green and white buoys. Coots shout, ducks sleep on a fat floating pipe.

I remember that I won't be able to say 'happy new year' to you tomorrow. But, also, that I will, anyway.

I remember that this will be the first year that you won't see, since 1989.

I remember that you didn't care for NYE. Who does?

I remember that you didn't like gin and tonics: gin, sure, but hold the tonic.

I remember that you had a *lot* of bikinis and very few pairs of shoes.

I remember the time you developed necrosis in your thigh due to a spider bite.

I remember that there were at least a dozen ways in which you might have died, or been killed. Why this one? Why not the destroyed sinking battleship?

I remember that Mrs Robertson, aka 'The Rob', English teacher for the ages, also died last year.

I remember that last spring the swans laid ten beautiful blue-grey eggs, but not a single cygnet survived more than two weeks after hatching.

I remember that I don't want to say goodbye to the year in which you died, the last you saw, and that I can't bring myself to say hello to a year that you won't see.

I remember how much you and I enjoyed reading and sharing one-star movie reviews (often to the point of actually watching the movie in question).

I remember Martin picking me up, when I was feeling blue, and saying that he had a hunch I just needed to get my feet off the ground for a moment or two.

I remember your method of eating peas, when forced to as a kid: one at a time, like tablets, with water.

I remember how you and dad loved to tell the story of the time I fainted in the surgery, when Chui the ginger tabby was being treated for maggots in a wound. I saw the maggots – fat, white, writhing lazily under a huge flap of skin – and immediately passed out, down down down onto the surgery floor, before shouting 'don't touch me!' as I came round. You and dad found this hilarious and the story became an instant family classic. I'm not even squeamish.

I remember 'the fucking sky .../ Every day its ego gets bigger and you let that happen' (Morgan Parker).

I remember: 'A demon has come and taken him away', from

the epic of Gilgamesh, as Gilgamesh mourns for Enkidu.

I remember how alarmingly creaky your knees were.

I remember trying to teach you to do a horse plait on yourself on Zoom.

I remember the time you and Hilda and Frankie came to Kenya for NYE at Diani – how you three were the naughtiest, coolest, sexiest girls I'd ever seen, and how I would have given anything to be even halfway like you.

I remember 'Bella ciao, bella ciao, bella ciao, ciao, ciao'.

I remember how strong you used to get from hauling air tanks in and out of boats and up and down beaches.

I remember Melville's description of the 'Huzza Porpoise': 'They are the lads that always live before the wind. They are accounted a lucky omen'.

I remember: 'text me when you get to Whitechapel and I'll meet you at Bow Road'.

I remember walking you to the tube station, a ten minute walk.

I remember walking to the tube station to meet you. I remember meeting you on the walk from/to the tube station, because Whitechapel is not ten minutes away from Bow Road at all.

I remember I'll never cram on a sweaty Central line with you again, en route to some bar or restaurant, just the two of us.

I remember you'll never ride the Elizabeth line.

I remember walking you to the tube station in freezing weather, so you could wear a coat for as long as possible before starting your journey to sunnier climes.

I remember: 'say hello to Kim for me' (Martin, as I leave for Panama, to send you off and collect your things).

I remember, this is the hardest and saddest thing I've ever done.

I remember sandwich bags for your ashes, and little plastic pots.

I remember I don't know what ashes look or feel like.

I remember, not very many times, flying back to England, to school, together, all three of us, seated in a row.

I remember that all the way to Panama there is a spare seat next to us, as if you had just popped to the loo.

I remember how little you were at Turi, and I remember Sophie telling me that other people had had that same memory of you too.

I remember the ocean. I remember waves. I remember 'water that cold feels like a thousand knives, stabbing you all over your body' *(Titanic)*.

I remember my promise to myself: when I get back from Panama, I'll swim once a week, in different bodies of water.

I remember that we never got to dive together again after Little Corn, though we always planned to – that the nearest I can get to doing this now is to dive where your ashes are scattered.

I remember: 'when the whole world hurts you bite it, don't you?' (Stephen Graham Jones).

I remember that in travelling to Panama we are making the same journey you did.

I remember *My Octopus Teacher*.

I remember that I'm wearing a top you gave me, and carrying a dry bag that you gave Martin.

I remember that you wanted a tattoo, but couldn't ever decide on what to get. I guess I'll get one for you.

I remember our mutual love of *Lost* (especially our mutual love of Sawyer).

I remember that you took this same bus trip – saw the same trees, frigate birds and vultures soaring, dried banana salespeople, cattle, distant green hills and water.

I remember that you were here.

I remember that you once worked in a spider monkey sanctuary.

I remember that we always used to drink a Tusker (usually followed by a bottle of red wine) whenever you came to London.

I remember drinking Tuskers in a pub in Covent Garden, followed by tapas and Spanish beers at a cute little bar just off the Strand.

I remember that Sophie and I flew over the Atlantic, the Gulf of Mexico, and the Caribbean Sea to come and say goodbye to you.

I remember that Panama, and Panamanian people, were good to you.

I remember Bob Dylan singing about a Panama hat.

I remember that you didn't really get Bob Dylan – that 'Bobby D' was more of a 'me and Sophie thing'.

I remember climbing the island tower in Little Corn. I remember your terrible vertigo.

I remember how much I want this trip to be over, how much I want to be home. I don't know how to say goodbye because I don't think I really believe you're gone.

I remember that we never managed to visit you here while you were alive – I remember 'under different circumstances'. I remember – I wonder if we'll ever come back.

I remember the store our bus drove past: Mini Super Kim.

I remember that you travelled back this way too, dead, in an ambulance, back to Santiago – up and down the hills, over the potholes, past the trees, the cattle (which look like Kenyan cattle), the brightly-painted bungalows, the flowers. What was that like? Who was with you? Were you alone?

I remember that you lived here. I keep expecting to see you, to hear your voice. It feels inconceivable that I am here, that we are here, and you are not. That we are here *because* you are not.

The sun is setting over the water, the sky streaked with scattered cloud, grey above me, pink and orange to my right. I remember that I really, *really* miss you.

I remember the three of us running down the beach into the sea at Vipingo.

I remember, on the drive to the coast, catching our first glimpse of 'the Finger', or Tudor Creek – proof, at last, that we really were nearly at Mombasa.

I remember: 'before we do anything else, we're going in the sea'.

I remember that all around us, here in Santa Catalina, are people who knew you, and yet I don't recognize any of them.

I remember that tomorrow I have to give your eulogy, read your elegy, in front of these people. I hope you're somewhere listening. I'm sorry in advance for my terrible Spanish.

I remember that Anthony cried at every third word when

giving his speech at Emma's wedding.

I remember that tomorrow Sophie and I will collect your things, and heft your heavy bag up the hill, the way you used to do.

I remember the smell of the sea.

I remember that we look alike – I wonder if anyone who knows you has seen me. Might they mistake me for your ghost, pale as I am?

I remember that you walked these roads, this beach; that you spent thousands of hours under this sea.

I remember how much you enjoyed a hammock.

I remember the feeling of sand under feet, slipping away as a wave recedes.

I remember paddling. I remember wet trouser legs.

I remember sunshine, thirty-degree heat, banana trees.

I remember meeting Sabina, your boss, outside the Panama Dive Center, holding each other, crying. Her slightly South African accent, her slim, tanned legs and bare feet, her tattoos. My pale feet on the tarmac beside hers as we walk up the hill.

I remember Las Hamacas. I remember swimming in the small pool. I remember that some people sitting by the pool had a very sick puppy. I wondered if we would have to watch him die. I couldn't bear it and went back to our hut – but a few minutes later he perked up and was walking around shakily on the grass.

I remember deep fried banana and pinto beans and Coke.

I remember the sounds of tropical birds and insects.

I remember sunset at around 5.30.

I remember your whale sharks.

I remember the evening breeze off the ocean.

I remember beach dogs, beach cats, beach chickens.

I remember our swim, mine and Soph's, first thing in the morning, in the sea by Town Beach, as the sun rose over the trees. The water was flat and quiet, the tide gentle. No one around. We felt that this is a beautiful, good place, and that there are beautiful, good people here.

I remember meeting Cedric and Camilo – the tight, tearful hugs of these careful, kind men.

I remember Sophie telling me that Michelle told her that you were found beside the bed; that you were very still, but somehow peaceful.

I remember that there's a black cat here with a voice exactly like Little Friend's.

I remember Lola, the dive shop dog, and Spliffy, the dive shop kitty, who lies fatly, white and un-dead, blind in one eye, on the dive shop counter.

I remember that Sabina would assuage your daily grumpiness by thrusting Spliffy into your arms first thing each morning.

I remember that you only had one pair of flipflops, and that no one knows where they went.

I remember swimming in the surf with Soph and Sabina, with Lola watching carefully from the shallows.

I remember sorting through your stuff. Your mountain of bikinis, your Superga, your Joni jeans, your tatty t-shirts and beleaguered denim cut-offs. The clothes we will keep to wear and keep to keep.

I remember the noodles and Coke we had, Sophie and I, sitting on our veranda, before we looked through your things.

I remember seeing your urn, and then your ashes, in Sabina and Camilo's house. How your ashes were grey and gritty, and abundant, and oddly somehow *you*. Hello there. I remember that I wasn't afraid of them, or even sad. I remember using a spoon to scoop you up, three of four spoons, into the little bag I'd brought to take you home in.

I remember the blue iridescent starling who dipped in the pool while we talked about the last conversations we'd had with you, and the things we were grateful for.

I remember that sorting through your clothes felt a little bit like going to mutumba in Nakuru.

I remember how I lifted your tatty grey jumper to my face, to smell it, hoping to smell you, and only smelling the mustiness of a jumper that had been in a bag, in a hot, damp climate, for over twelve weeks.

I remember that today is Sophie's birthday. I give her a silver bracelet with a knot on it. I remember you teaching us to tie underwater knots in Little Corn. The sheet (sheep) bend.

I remember that Sabina found a dead turtle on the beach on the morning of your death – before she found you.

I remember learning that a lot of people waited with you until the police and ambulance came – for over five hours. Sabina, Michelle, Solin, and others. I remember worrying that you were alone. I remember that you were here, in this beautiful place, among friends.

I remember that the send-off we held for you on Town Beach was at sunset. That there were dogs there, and your friends.

I remember many hugs.

I remember how much my hands shook as I read my eulogy and how I couldn't look at anyone.

I remember that Sophie and I hugged at the end.

I remember your urn, laid out on the rocks, on a kanga, the

incoming tide growing ever closer, the darkness falling.

I remember the little cauldron we used to burn our messages to you.

I remember how much everyone cried. How Camilo couldn't stop.

I remember meeting Solin. I remember hugging him, and giving him, uselessly, a little pewter cat, and telling him, as Michelle translated, that he was part of our family.

I remember Tara's beautiful talk about you; her references to lyrics from Garth Brooks and a quotation by Sylvia Earle, along with something that you had written in one of your dive logs, by someone called Randy Komisar: 'the most dangerous risk of all: the risk of spending your life not doing what you want on the bet you can buy yourself the freedom to do it later'.

I remember dinner afterwards, with Cedric and Alaina, Mike and Michelle, Sabina and Camilo: I had a gin cocktail and a Thai red curry. I sat next to Camilo and Sophie, Michelle sat opposite. I remember someone's lovely little dog.

I remember not being able to sleep.

I remember, the next morning, the boat to Coiba, sitting between Sophie and Camilo as we chugged slowly out through the mangroves in the early morning sun, Kat, Sabina, and Michelle in a row behind us, Solin sitting with the boat captain, Lorenzo, in the stern. Then the choppy, beautiful water, the flying fish, the mainland running greenly to our right.

I remember the ranger's station, and the three spotted eagle rays swimming near the beach.

I remember the huge crocodile half-sleeping in the creek.

I remember the dolphins.

I remember collecting sand from two beaches, one white, the other volcanic.

I remember saying 'bye Bimble' as Sophie poured your ashes into the water, the boat moving slowly over your favourite dive site, Buffet, in the Gulf of Chiriquí. I remember lifting two handfuls of ash and throwing them in the water. We threw flowers, earrings, and a pebble. The ashes bubbled a little, and the sun shone deep into the water, in spears of white-ish light. I remember the dive that followed. Solin, Sabina, Camilo, Kat, and me.

I remember descending down the buoy line. I remember white tip reef sharks, big ones, lazing about. I remember a big old turtle, gamely bashing something huge and orange against the sea floor, holding it between her flippers and nibbling the debris. I remember that small yellow fish gathered around her, to feast on any leftovers. I remember morays, parrot fish, puffers, and angels.

I remember that on sinking backwards into the ocean the water itself seems to disappear, to be transformed into a kind of thick blue light. It's hard to imagine that what surrounds you is wet, heavy, capable of waves and spray, constantly in motion, a marker of horizon; that only a little further down it amounts to a sustained force of unsurvivable pressure.

I remember the poem that Erin re-wrote, an oceanic version of 'Do Not Stand at My Grave and Weep', which Sabina read twice, first in English and then in Spanish:
> *Don't scatter my ashes and weep,*
> *For I'm not there.*
> *I sure don't sleep.*
> *I am the tidal constant flow,*
> *I am the turtles deep below.*
> *I am the strength in mantas' wings,*
> *I am the humpback whale that sings.*
> *In the reef with those puffer fish*
> *I am at peace; your eternal wish.*
> *In black rocks with the white tip shark,*
> *I am love, in both light and dark.*
> *Don't hang your rig and question why,*
> *I am not there,*
> *I did not die.*

I remember wearing your fins and your dive computer and hoping you would be proud of my buoyancy control.

I remember assuring Sophie that we would never forget you – not even the little things; especially not the little things.

I remember the card that Sophie and the kids made to send you, along with two riotous photos of you with the kids: they never sent it to you, so we opened it on our little veranda at Las Hamacas, the morning before we sent you off.

I remember walking with Michelle across Town Beach, through the creek where you once fell on your ass and drowned your phone, and up the hill to Bluezone, to your old house, a little bungalow painted bright blue.

I remember learning that three people had drowned that day on Santa Catalina's other beach.

I remember the three cats that chased each other through Las Hamacas.

Three cats, three eagle rays, three deaths, three sisters.

I remember Julie, the diving instructor who we met on the beach of a small island in Coiba, and again at a restaurant in the evening, who spoke so highly of you.

I remember thinking: I will return to this place.

I remember that I wish I could tell you all about our trip. That we met all these people who knew you and loved you, that I dived where you dived, saw your sharks, travelled to Coiba in your boat with your boat captain, your friends and colleagues, endured the same smack of the surf on the way back to the mainland and the same achy back that followed.

I remember that you could have been there at dinner, laughing along at the stories we told about you.

I remember the depthless despair that I carry, that hasn't gone away.

I remember that grief, like the ocean, is something not to be mastered or survived but to be navigated.

I remember that St. Brendan of Clonfert is the patron saint of sailors, divers, adventurers, travellers, and whales.

I remember that diving is a poetic act, pivoting on creativity and control.

I remember that some fish move like birds, in murmurations.

I remember the breath taken; the ascent.

I remember that no one offers medication for chronic crying.

I remember that sometimes I don't think my family likes me very much; I remember thinking that you did.

I remember the weight of emptiness.

I remember washing your clothes on our return from Panama. Hanging them up. Being surrounded by material evidence that you had existed, here and not here.

I remember that I put all the cards and little gifts people sent me, along with your documents – your passports, ID card, PADI licenses – and my London Marathon medal, into the heavy-duty plastic bag that contained your ashes. Now everything is covered with a fine layer of ash, including my fingers.

I remember planting the rambling rose in your memory, by

the old factory chimney, near our bird feeders – a rose that I hope will grow to be large and strong, sharp and beautiful, that will nourish and shelter birds and insects. I planted it at dusk, in January, digging a hole with my small wood-handled trowel and my hands, Lady observing nearby. In the hole, I sprinkled some of your ashes. Grow, rose, grow.

I remember transferring some of your ashes and some sand from Coiba, still wet, into the little glass bottle that Michelle had given me, decorated with shells and a turtle.

I remember that I carried some of your ashes home with me in a small Chanel make-up bag.

I remember, one winter evening, going upstairs, opening the cubed, carved wooden jewellery box into which I'd placed you, lifting you out, and holding you in my hand. All that's left, etc. Inside the Chanel bag, a small plastic baggie. You look like drugs. I rolled the bag between my fingers and thumb; held it up to the light, the better to contemplate that curious mix of fine grey ash and little hunks of black and white matter.

I remember: 'we who are about to die salute thee!'

I remember: I never knew how a death could bring some people together, whilst driving others apart.

I remember: all I want to do is talk about you, and everyone assumes that I want to do anything but.

I remember that every day I go running in your UnderArmour sports bra.

I remember that the sand I brought back from Coiba and Catalina is in a little metal velvet-lined pot that Dolla gave me.

I remember that the ocean is not empty.

I remember that there is no horizon under water.

I remember: 'Heart First'.

I remember that I've dreamed about you every night for the past three nights.

I remember that you'll never, now, come back to live in London.

I remember: 'isn't every ending absolute to those who live through it?' (Jessie Greengrass)

I remember that you used to swim at a lido somewhere in North London, but I can't remember where.

I remember feeling messy, untethered, and going for a swim in the Hackney Reservoir. I realised that the nearest tube station to the reservoir is Manor House, near where you used to live. I remember meeting you there, the station with many exits, filled with garbage and a hot wind, and then walking down Green Lanes with you. I retraced our steps and immersed myself in the cold brown water.

I remember: 'How lost can you be when everywhere you turn it's morning & the sun's coming up' (Mayer).

I remember 'thoughts that do often lie too deep for tears' (Wordsworth).

I remember that it's five nights now I've dreamed dreams shaped by your death.

I remember the dream in which you weren't dead after all; you just needed some space. There you were, alive, living by a river, blonde and wearing shorts and just needing some space.

I remember how you used to drink a glass of warm water every morning, first thing.

I remember 'let us, then, be up and doing / with a heart for any fate!' (Longfellow).

I remember: 'He is not here, but far away / The noise of life begins again, / And ghastly thro' the drizzling rain / On the bald street breaks the blank day' (Tennyson).

I remember: 'But grief is darker. / It is a wig / that does not rest gently / on my head' (Essex Hemphill).

I remember all the people – strangers, friends, family – involved when someone dies.

I remember there are cracks in all directions.

I remember – I want someone else to die. Not someone close to me. Someone close to someone else.

I remember more dreams.

I remember 'reeling'.

I remember 'undone'.

I remember wondering, watching some horror film with Martin, what you'd sound like if you talked to us through a medium – what kind of voice you'd assume (to scare us), and what kinds of things you'd make the medium do.

I remember how I used to quite like *not* hearing from you for a while, because it usually meant you were having a good time and were too busy being happy to message me.

I remember: 'The longer / the life the more lives / are accumulated' (Edmund Berrigan).

I remember how much you loved Rafa Nadal – how we always cheered his wins together and felt sad about his losses; how much I want to tell you about his win in Melbourne.

I remember: 'Write from what hurts you; investigate what gives you pain; seek your community there' (Stephanie Burt).

I remember I have been reconfigured. My family has been reconfigured. My memories – all reconfigured.

I remember: 'it felt as though her problems were on the surface of the earth again, not down in its molten core' (Yaa Gyasi).

I remember that no one can feel about this the way that I feel about it – only I am me.

I remember the infinite failures of language.

I remember: 'I see pride! I see power!' *(Cool Runnings)*.

I remember 'the seeing hands of others' (Frank O'Hara).

I remember elegy: 'I push it around trying / to make it say / what I want it to say' (Mark Bibbins).

I remember you were born in a December and died in an October.

I remember 'the sharpest edges of grief'.

I remember – I wonder what it felt like to die.

I remember, again – how did you actually die? Why did your heart stop beating? What is meant by 'acute metabolic disorder'?

I remember: 'There are days when everything / feels like a metaphor / for your having died // There are days / when nothing does' (Mark Bibbins).

I remember how exhausting it is to see people, because of my autopilot, and the aftermath, loquacious demon, intruding on my quietness.

I remember – we must live each moment to the full because you can't.

I remember – easier said than done.

I remember how much I hate the language of grief – getting *over*, moving *on*, going *through*. The day you died is a day time stopped. I'm always there. It's always here.

I remember: perhaps I can learn to accommodate it.

I remember I can do whatever I want to make myself feel better.

I remember: 'You must speak not only of great devastation' (Ilya Kaminsky).

I remember: 'I am not deaf. I simply told the world to shut off its crazy noise for a while' (Ilya Kaminsky).

I remember how much, sometimes, I dread seeing other people. I remember that socialising now leaves me with a week of headache, and not being able to eat.

I remember meeting, or encountering, other bereaved.

I remember you and me reading on our beds all day.

I remember when you were about eleven and what you wanted more than anything was a valance around your bed.

I remember – what I feel is unique to me because only I knew you in the way that I knew you. I remember 'you do not always know what I am feeling' (O'Hara).

Choosing between two numbered bamboo toothbrushes – 4 and 5 – I choose 5, because we are a family of 5. Then I remember. Are we? Should I have chosen 4? I stick with 5.

I remember a letter arriving for you, sixteen weeks after your death, reminding you to book a smear test. I remember thinking 'at least you never have to go through *that* again' and hearing you laugh.

I remember 'wake up and live!' (Langston Hughes).

I remember: 'as a condition of being, as a kind of meaning, as a direction taken' (Nick Cave).

I remember 'I don't want to leave a messy corpse' (Jericho Brown). I bet your corpse was beautifully un-messy. And beautifully beautiful. I bet you looked hot, even in death.
I remember that I am so grateful for your presence on this earth – that I knew you, that you were my sister.

I remember: 'memory is a reflection of self' (Sarah Schulman).

I remember: 'our disappeared friends have taken our fear with them' (Sarah Schulman).

I remember: 'There's no marker. Just our hearts. We know where he is' (Jill Kelloran).

I remember a dream in which we're in Santa Catalina, and you're dead but also there, a ghost made flesh, and I have to stop you from going to the dive shop to say hello to Sabina, because you're dead, and I don't know how to explain this to you.

I remember, in the same dream, telling you about your Santa Catalina funeral.

I remember: why should I survive where you didn't?

I remember: 'Thinking about the moments that won't happen is hard, too' (Herbert Muschamp).

I remember everything you won't ever do, and its unendurable.

I remember 'the heat and confusion of living, which is the only answer to death' (Audre Lorde).

I remember realising that the inaugural poetry reading of the Network for New York School Studies took place on October 9th. Just nine days later, you died.

I remember how wild your eyes used to look – as if you were really, really high – after your diabetes eye health check-up at Mile End.

I remember that it has been sixteen weeks, then seventeen, then twenty, then – when a dear friend announces her pregnancy – an eerie twenty-four.

I remember: 'The anger, too. How dare they die. And leave us alone to deal with all this shit. With no one to complain to' (Herbert Muschamp).

I remember Sacha's Place, a bench in Victoria Park with a plaque on it that reads: 'All welcome. Rest. Be easy. You are safe. Love lives here'.

I remember 'the story blows away / And what can you do, howling without a script?' (Ashbery).

I remember how much of this I've remembered, and written, whilst on tube journeys to see friends.

I remember almost everyone will experience grief. That those of us who do are the lucky ones. To have loved. To continue to live.

I remember that the pandemic has bereaved the world. That I am just one of a number.

I remember the bodies I have seen. The man on the Nakuru highway in Lanet, hit by a car. Nonna, in her lovely makeup and funeral regalia. Aki the brown cat, cruelly dead under the bridge in the pre-dawn drizzle. I did not see your body, though I try to imagine what 'it' ('you') looked like all the time.

I wonder what your last moments were like. I wish I had had the opportunity to bathe your body, to prepare you for whatever came next, though neither of us believed that anything did. To talk to you. To enact some of the ease and familiarity, even after death, of sharing make-up tips, hair oil, perfume, each other's clothes. I wish I had been able to unfurl a clean white sheet around your body.

I remember imagining you watching the drama of your death unfold. I can't imagine you simply disappearing.

I remember: 'How could he be so present one moment and altogether gone the next? How could a life so strong be simply annihilated?' (David Gere).

I remember: 'It's not uncommon, the dead are frequently unable to accept their condition, they resemble the living in that respect, but they have forgotten what they're nostalgic for, much is lost in the crossing over' (Damon Galgut).

I remember: will I meet your ghost?

I remember that I keep a handful of your ashes as a talisman of memory and good luck.

I remember: 'They existed. They existed. / We can be' (Maya Angelou).

I remember: 'Why do I tell you these things? / You are not even here' (John Ashbery).

ACKNOWLEDGEMENTS

Thank you Stuart Bartholomew for taking a chance on this book.

Thank you my Martin, thank you Cousin and Lady, thank you Little Friend.

Thank you Sophie.

Thank you Dolla, Eloise, Amy, Joanna, Jess, Ben, Bean, Riley, Ali, Garry, Monty, Denise, Laura H., Sofie, Cindy, Rachel, Fariha, Dorothy, Asha, Sara, Dave, Rebecca, Sabina, Michelle, Yasmine, Bella, Steph, Sandra, Joe, Vanessa, Laura F., Paul, Martha, Ange, Fallon, Paolo, John, Mandana, Camilo, Fallon, Mark, Anne, Lindsay, Xaime.

ABOUT VERVE POETRY PRESS

Verve Poetry Press is a quite new and already prize-winning press that focused initially on meeting a local need in Birmingham - a need for the vibrant poetry scene here in Brum to find a way to present itself to the poetry world via publication. Co-founded by Stuart Bartholomew and Amerah Saleh, it now publishes poets from all corners of the UK - poets that speak to our city's varied and energetic qualities and will contribute to its many poetic stories.

Added to this is a colourful pamphlet series, many featuring poets who have performed at our sister festival - and a poetry show series which captures the magic of longer poetry performance pieces by festival alumni such as Polarbear, Matt Abbott and Imogen Stirling.

The press has been voted Most Innovative Publisher at the Saboteur Awards, and has won the Publisher's Award for Poetry Pamphlets at the Michael Marks Awards.

Like the festival, we strive to think about poetry in inclusive ways and embrace the multiplicity of approaches towards this glorious art.

www.vervepoetrypress.com
@VervePoetryPres
mail@vervepoetrypress.com